POVERTY IN NAGALAND

T. Zarenthung Ezung

AKANSHA PUBLISHING HOUSE
NEW DELHI • GUWAHATI • VISAKHAPATNAM

AKANSHA PUBLISHING HOUSE
4649-B/21, Ansari Road
Darya Ganj, New Delhi - 110 002
Ph.: 23263193 / 9811582579 / 09435116718
Fax: 011-23263193
Email: ektabooks@yahoo.com
www.akanshapublishinghouse.com

Poverty in Nagaland

First Published 2011
ISBN 978-81-8370-283-6

PRINTED IN INDIA

Published by Akansha Publishing House, New Delhi and Printed at Harmain Offset Press, Delhi.

Dedicated to

My Loving Father and Late Mother (Chichano)

Contents

Preface

Poverty is a man-made disease affecting and taking more tolls on human lives than the most dreaded HIV/AIDS in today's world. Nearly half of the population continues to live largely under the condition of subsistence agriculture and acute poverty. The analysis through multi-poverty index (MPI) reveals that 1.3 billion people live on USD 1.25 a day or less. Nagaland, the 16th state of Indian Union is no exception to other state when it comes to poverty. Nagaland, even after more than four decades of statehood, has 32.67 percent of people living below poverty line during 1999-00. Moreover, the phenomenon of poverty is dominant in the rural areas with 40.04% of people living below the poverty line as compared to 7.47% of the poor in urban areas. However, it is to be noted here that the poverty ratio of Assam is being used to measure the extent of poverty of Nagaland which is not appropriate. Thus, estimating the extent and depth of poverty in Nagaland based on its own norms becomes vital. The present work seeks to address the problem of poverty measurement in the state and to suggest certain remedial measure for this disease.

The whole work has been divided in six chapters. The statement of the problem, objectives, hypothesis and methodology of the study have been discussed in chapter I, whereas, Chapter II deals with the socio-economic condition of the state, district and the villages. Chapter III deals with the nutritional norms, monthly per capita expenditure (MPCE) and the relationship between family size and nutritional intake, MPCE. The extent and depth of poverty have been measured in chapter IV. Chapter V deals with the existence of inequalities in the distribution of nutritional intake and MPCE. Moreover, the relationship between the inequalities and proportion of the poor has been discussed in this chapter. In Chapter VI, the main findings are highlighted and the author has attempted to conclude by providing a roadmap for policy makers.

T. Zarenthung Ezung

Acknowledgements

This volume is a revised version of the doctoral dissertation submitted to the department of Economics, Nagaland University (NU). The author has done his research work on *"Nutrition and Poverty Assessment in Nagaland: A Case Study of Wokha district"*.

Through this, I would like to express my profound gratitude and indebtedness to several people who have helped me directly or indirectly in the completion of this book.

Firstly I thank the almighty God for his blessing and my father, late mother, brothers, in-laws, my loving wife Renchano and kids for their unfailing support.

I am grateful to Dr. B. Kilangla Jamir, Associate Professor, Department of Economics, Nagaland University, for her guidance and supervision throughout my research work.

Special thanks to the faculty Department of Economics, Nagaland University, Dr. M.K. Sinha, Dr. Temjenzulu Jamir, Dr. Giribabu M. and Miss Alice for their support and help.

I am also indebted to Dr. A.C. Dubey, NCEAR for his help. I would like to thank Mr. Mhonchan Ezung for being with me during my field survey. Special thanks to Mr. Likhase Sangtam, Mr. Charles Kikon, Respondents and host of friends for their help during my research work.

I also thank Dr. Kedilezo Kikhi, and Dr. Athungo Ovung, Department of Sociology, N.U. for their help, advice and inspiration during the course of this book.

Lastly, Mr. M. P. Misra of Akansha Publishing House, New Delhi deserves special thanks for agreeing to bring out my research work in this book format.

T. Zarenthung Ezung

Mokokchung
June 2011

List of Tables

List of Figures

1

Introduction

This chapter deals with the concepts and issues relating to nutrition norms and poverty lines. The problems, universe, periods and methodology of the study has been highlighted. Moreover, the chapter also discussed the objectives and hypothesis of the study.

Introduction and Concepts

Poverty is man's powerful and massive affliction. It is the progenitor of much pain from hunger and disease onto civil war and conflict itself.[1] Nearly half of the world populations continue to live largely under the condition of subsistence agriculture and acute poverty. A poverty curtain has descended right across the face of the world, dividing it materially and philosophically into two different worlds – one embarrassingly rich and the other desperately poor. This invisible barrier exists within nations as well as between them, and it often provides unity of thought and purpose to the third world countries which otherwise have their economic, political and cultural differences. "The struggle to lift this curtain is certainly the most formidable challenge of our time".[2] Over the ages, a culture of poverty has got transmitted from generation to generation in India. Poverty here is not a pathological deviation from the normal and normative but the state of affairs and the set of conditions under which the overwhelming majority of the people are compelled to live. "Backwardness here has often been characterized by a syndrome of collective poverty".[3] In India planning was adopted in the early 1950's but the necessity and urge for planning was openly expressed during the later half of the previous century. Leading nationalist wrote extensively on pauperization, famine and abject poverty among the masses. Thus "poverty has been our continuing preoccupation since the colonial period."[4] Therefore, it is natural to expect from our planners under the leadership of Nehru to give top priority to poverty and consequently the introduction of poverty alleviation programme in the planning process.

The definition of poverty is related to people's living standard. Poverty is human condition characterized by the sustained or chronic deprivation of the resources, capabilities, choices, security and power necessary for the enjoyment of an adequate standard of living; others include civil, cultural, economic, political and social rights (World Health Organization 2004).[5] According to Sen (1992), 'Poverty is the failure of basic capabilities to reach certain minimally acceptable levels. The functioning's relevant to this can vary from such elementary physical ones as being well-nourished, being adequately clothed and sheltered, avoiding preventable morbidity, etc., to more complex social achievements such as taking part in the life of the community, being able to appear in public without shame, and so on'. Poverty exists when individuals or groups are not able to satisfy their basic needs adequately.[6] This view maintains that poverty has three aspects of want of material goods or materialistic possession: (i) those necessary to avoid suffering and needed to fulfill the requirements of hunger and shelter, that is, those needed to survive, (ii) such as are essential to meet human needs of health, that is, to get nutrition and to avoid disease, and (iii) those needed to maintain a minimum subsistence level. In simple term, this refers to minimum amount of food intake, adequate housing, clothing, education and health care.[7] A similar definition put forwarded by Dubey and Sarma (2000)[8] states that the concept of poverty is related to deprivation perceived by a civic society with respect to the basic minimum needs.

Recent quantitative assessment on poverty distinguishes between absolute and relative poverty. Poverty can be defined objectively and applied consistently only in terms of the concept of relative deprivation. Individuals families and groups in the population can be said to be in poverty when they lack the resources to obtain the types of diet, participate in the activities and have the living conditions and amenities which are customary, or at least widely encouraged or approved, in the societies to which they belong. Their resources are so seriously below those commanded by the average individual or family that they are, in fact, excluded from ordinary living patterns, customs or activities.[9] Thus, at the core of relative poverty is inequality. The relative poverty takes into account relative deprivation rather than the absolute deprivation. In this sense, relative poverty essentially compares the deprivation of the people at the lower end of distribution to those of the higher end. Therefore, in relative sense, a person might be above the socially perceived minimum level of economic welfare but she/he will be considered poor in relative sense. The direct measure of inequality look at the cumulative distribution of income or consumption and estimate the extent to which it deviates from a norm of perfect equality. "The most preferred index is Gini Index". The absolute poverty is based on socially perceived deprivation, where one or more members of the population in a predefined universe fail to fulfill their minimum basic needs. The common approach in measuring absolute poverty is to specify a bundle of goods and services deemed necessary to meet basic consumption needs. "The most widely used estimates use food requirements to define basic consumption needs".[10] There are many scholars who define poverty interms of basic minimum consumption or nutrition. Horwitz (1997)[11] states that "Poverty breeds malnutrition and, in turn, malnutrition increases poverty, a vicious circle". Thus, poverty also means malnutrition, hunger and food poverty. Hunger is "a craving or need for food" and malnutrition is "faulty or imperfect nutrition".[12] Hunger Task Force (2003),[13] defines hunger as a condition in which people lack the basic food intake to provide them with the energy and nutrients for fully productive lives. Dasgupta (1993)[14] states that hunger is measured in terms of availability, access or intake of calories relative to caloric requirements that varies principally by age, sex and activity levels. Friel (2004)[15] defines food poverty as the inability to access a nutritionally adequate diet and related impacts on health culture and social participation. Thus, the interlinkage between poverty and nutrition cannot be ignored. Nutritional intake and status is both the effect and a cause of income earning opportunities of the individuals and households. As an out come, the nutritional status of individuals is influenced, among other things, by the amount and type of food that is consumed. A given level of income may be distributed differently by household between food and non-food items, which, in turn, will affect the nutritional outcome of a given levels of income.[16] In India, the expert group on poverty appointed by the Planning Commission in 1993 had recommended that the definition of poverty be extended to include deprivation in basic needs such as education, health and shelter as also other basic amenities such as drinking water. However, not much progress has been made in widening the definition of poverty in India.[17]

Poverty Line and Nutritional Norms

Now the pertinent question that arises here is, then, what is the actual nutritional requirement or income of the people to be considered as non-poor? Poverty is determined by the standard that exists within the society. Poverty is perceived in terms of poverty line, which is determined by the prevailing standard of what is needed for health, efficiency, nurturing of children, social participation and the maintenance of self-respect.[18] Thus, defining poverty line becomes the first step in estimating poverty. A poverty line dividing the poor from non-poor is used, by putting a price on the minimum required consumption level of foods.[19] The major components of food are carbohydrates, proteins, fats, vitamins and minerals. These foods give the nutritional requirement of the people measured in terms of calorie.[20] The total expenditure on both food and non-food divided by the population gives the poverty line. However, academic studies in the early 1970's generated a rich and extensive literature on poverty based on, or related to, the poverty line. The result was greater data availability, increasing methodological sophistication, and emerging concerns and insights. Thus while deriving poverty lines, it was recognized that human existence is more than just food, and provision for other goods and services also needed to be made. Since there are no a priori norms for these, it was felt that the actual expenditure of the households should form the basis for estimating the necessary expenditure on these goods and services.[21] In the literature of economics these topics have been vastly debated and examined by many scholars and government agencies.

Deaton (2000) analysed the World Bank Report 2000 estimates of poverty line basing on 1993 purchasing power parities at $ 1.08 a day per person, but is still conveniently referred to as the $1 a day poverty line. The World Bank's worldwide count of the poor starts from a common international poverty line and counts the number of people in each country whose consumption lies below it. The international poverty line, at $1-or $2-a-day is converted into domestic currencies using purchasing power parity exchange rates. But he is of the view that, although the $1-a-day common line has much to recommend it, its dependence on purchasing power parity exchange rates has a number of drawbacks. Thus he suggested that, a better procedure for the future would be to hold fixed (in real terms) the current domestic poverty lines, and not to revise them along with changes in PPP exchange rates induced by updating of base years.

World Bank Report (2001), shows that malnutrition afflicts an estimated 62 million children in all States. Estimates, during the mid-1990s shows that more than half of the children belonging to age group of 1-5 years old in rural areas in 12 out of the 14 larger Indian States are undernourished, with more girl children tending to suffer severe malnutrition. Chronic energy deficiency also persists among adults. In several large states, over 40-50% of adults suffer from chronic energy deficiency. The results of the National Sample Survey Organization 1993-94 quinquennial consumer expenditure survey, used to roughly approximate nutritional intake, suggest that the poorest 25% of the rural population consumed on average 1,900 calories or less per day, in contrast to the average recommended daily allowance (RDA) of 2400 calories. The poorest 25% of the urban population consumed on average 1,700 calories per day or less, compared to the average recommended daily allowance (RDA) of 2,100 calories. The report showed that this is due to inefficiency in implementing programmes that are meant for the poor as well as the inefficiency of the public distribution system.

Oberg (2003) explained how poor are being defined. He shows that, the Census Bureau uses a set of money income thresholds that vary by family size and composition to establish the official measure of poverty line in the U.S. Thus, the poverty line was fixed at an annual income of $9,214 in 2001 for a single person, $12207 for family of two, $14269 for family of three, $18,022 for family of four, $20812 for family of five, $23221 for family of six, $25462 for family of seven, $28893 for family of eight and $34238 for family of nine. With the poverty line, he analysed the trends of the overall poverty rate in the U.S. from 1959 to 2001. His analysis shows that, in 1960, 35% of the population —over 5 million people— were poor, with the elderly comprising the largest segment. Since then, there has been a significant reduction in the number of elderly persons living in poverty to a rate of 10.1% in 2001. After 1975, the rate continued a steady decline for those over 65 years, while it increased for children. The poverty rate for children rose to an all time high of 22% in 1982 and again in 1993 equaling the rates observed in the 1960s. Despite a reduction in the childhood poverty rate since 1993, in part due to the strong economy of the 1990s, children remain disproportionately represented among poor Americans, with a rate of 16.3% in 2001.

FAO 2005, evaluated the availability of basic food and accessibility to those foods and to basic nutritional elements in rural India. The crucial findings of this paper revealed that as the farm size decreases, calorie intake per person decreases. They also showed us that junk of the poor are in the marginal and sub-marginal holding of farm. As regards to under nourishment, the paper clearly showed that sub-marginal farm household contributed for 46.9% of the total undernourishment of the rural farm households.

Poverty line in the context of India was first mooted by the Indian Labour Conference in 1957. The definition of poverty line was attempted first in 1962 by a working group of eminent economists and social thinkers after taking into account the recommendation of the Indian Council of Medical Research (ICMR, 1958). They recommended that the national minimum for each household of 5 persons should not be less than Rs. 100 per month in terms of 1960-61 prices or Rs. 20 per capita. This national minimum excludes expenditure on health and education, both of which are expected to be provided by the state according to the constitution and in the light of its other commitments.

In the late sixties, Ojha (1970)[22] defined poverty in terms of basic minimum needs, which in turn, were expressed in terms of physical survival. According to him, the minimum calories requirement was 2250 per day per person. In terms of foodgrains (pulses and cereals) minimum calories required were 1500 and 1800 for urban and rural areas respectively. Minimum calorie intake was then expressed in terms of physical quantities of food grains. He estimated 518 grams per day per person for rural areas and 432 grams per day per capita urban areas. He defined poverty line at Rs. 15-18 (at 1960-61 prices) per capita per month for rural population and Rs. 8-11 per capita per month for urban population. On the basis of these minima, he estimated that in 1960-61, 51.8% of rural population and 7.6% of urban population are below poverty line.

One of the earliest and very comprehensive studies was made by Dandekar and Rath (1971).[23] According to this study group, the average calorie norm is 2250 calories per capita per day for both the rural and urban areas. They suggested that whereas the Planning Commission accepts Rs. 20 per capita per month (Rs. 240 per annum) as the minimum desirable standard, it would not be fair to use this figure for both rural and urban areas. On the basis of the NSSO data on consumer expenditure, they revealed that, in rural area, the households with monthly per capita of Rs.14.20 at 1960-61 prices and consumed on an average food with calorie equivalent to 2250 per capita per day together with such non-food items as they chose. The corresponding figures in the urban area were Rs. 22.50 per capita per month at 1960-61 prices. On average a per capita monthly expenditure of Rs. 20 (at 1960-61 prices) was deemed to be the national minimum. On the basis of these minima, they estimated that in 1960-61, 40% of rural population and 50% of urban population are below poverty line.

Bardhan (1973), defined poverty line to be monthly per capita income of Rs. 15 at 1960-61 prices for the rural people. He noted that 53% of the rural population were below the poverty line.[24] Minhas (1978)[25] does not split the minimum requirements to draw the poverty line between rural and urban areas. He defines poverty line in terms of minimum amount of per capita consumption expenditure. He refers to a distinguished study group constituted in july 1962 comprising D.R. Gadgil, B.N. Ganguli, P.S. Lokanathan, M.R. Masani, Asoka Mehta, Shriman Narayan, Pitambar Pant, V.K.R.V. Rao, and Anna Saheb Sahasrabudha which recommended a standard of private consumption of Rs. 240 (at 1960-61 prices) per capita per year bare minimum. For rural areas, Minhas suggested that, the poverty line may be drawn at Rs. 200 per capita per year. The World Bank in its study on India's poverty used alternative method of estimating poverty proportions applying a deflator series developed by NSS and the Indian Statistical Institute to calculate updated poverty lines in current prices. The study showed that the poverty line is Rs. 55.2 for rural and Rs. 112.2 for urban for 1977-78 and Rs. 89 for rural and Rs. 68.6 for urban for 1983. On this basis, he estimated that in 1967-68, 37.1% of rural population and 50.6% of urban population are below poverty line.

A Task Force (1979) constituted by the Perspective Planning Division of Planning Commission adopted derivation of poverty line in the normative minimum calorie intake. This group accepted the calorie intake norms recommended by the Nutrition Expert Group (1968), according to fourteen age-sex-activity categories.

This provided the age-sex-activity-specific composition of the rural and urban populations. The specific calorie norms were then weighted by the corresponding compositions of the rural and urban populations separately, to derive the rural and urban average calorie norms. The daily calorie requirement per person was worked out, on average, to 2435 and 2095 calories in rural and urban India, respectively (GOI, 1979). Thus if the people living in rural and urban areas can afford to consume on average at least 2435 and 2095 calories of food per day, respectively, they are said to be above the poverty line. Further, the Planning Commission has also estimated the total expenditure of the food and non-food items for urban and rural areas: these expenditure levels became their respective poverty lines. At 1973 prices, the poverty lines for rural and urban areas stood at Rs 49 and Rs 57 per person per month respectively (GOI 1979). Currently, these figures stand at approximately Rs 368 and Rs 559 per person per month for rural and urban areas respectively (GOI 1993).

Likewise the estimate of Datt and Ravallion[26] (1989) gave the poverty line at Rs.89 and developed the concept of poverty gap. The Planning Commission constituted an Expert Group in September 1989 to consider methodological and computational aspects of estimation of proportion and number of poor in India. The poverty line recommended by the task force on projection of minimum needs and effective consumption demand, namely a monthly per capita total expenditure of Rs. 49.09 per month for rural areas and Rs. 56.64 per month for urban areas rounded respectively to Rs. 49 and Rs. 57 at all India level at 1973-74 prices. This was anchored in the recommended per capita daily intake of 2400 calories in the rural areas with reference to the consumption pattern as obtained in 1973-74.

Similarly, Dubey and Gangopadhyay (1998) taking the calorie intake as 2435 per capita per day for rural and 2095 per capita per day for urban areas and the poverty line of Rs. 49.09 for rural and Rs. 56.64 for urban areas as estimated by the Expert Group (1993), they re-estimated the poverty line. The re-estimated rural poverty line on the basis of a uniform calorie is 2250 per capita. The rural poverty line turned out to be the Per Capita Total Expenditure (PCTE) level of Rs. 15 per month at 1960-61 prices. Whereas, the urban poverty line at 1960-61 prices is reported to be Rs. 18 per capita per month.[27] As of 1990-2000, the poverty lines declared by the Planning Commission were Rs. 327 and Rs. 454 for rural and urban areas, respectively. The NSSO the 61st round 2004-05 estimated the calorie norms as 2047 Kcal for the rural areas and 2020 Kcal for urban areas, while the poverty line has been fixed at Rs. 558.78 at 2004-05 prices for rural areas and Rs. 1052 at the current prices for urban areas.

Meenakshi and Viswanathan (2003) in their analytical study reviews calorie deprivation in rural India for the year 1983 – 1999/ 2000. Their findings show that there is a decline in income poverty over the 1980's and 1990's and calorie deprivation in rural India has in fact increased. In 1983, average intakes were below 2400 calories in all but six states and were above the norm only in the northern region. By 1999-2000, intakes had declined in all states except Kerala, Orissa and West Bengal. However, the depth and severity of nutrient deprivation declined, as did the incidence of abject calorie deprivation. Using 2400 norm, their finding shows that the severity of calorie inadequacy increased only in four states, and declined in the remaining 12 states. Despite the apparent divergence between calorie- and income-poverty trends, income continues to be a powerful determinant of calorie intakes. Their estimates, based on a comparison of 1983 and 1993-94 intakes, indicated that calorie elasticities with respect to income were in the range of 0.5 to 0.7 for the poorest quintile in 1983, and were higher a decade later.

Deolalikar and Dubey (2003) examined both the incidence of hunger-poverty – as measured by the inadequacy of calorie intake – among Indian metropolitan cities (urban agglomerations) in 1999-2000 as well as the change in hunger-poverty between 1993-94 and 1999-2000. The recent evidence from India suggests a divergent trend in the incidence of consumption-poverty and hunger-poverty; while the headcount index of consumption poverty has steadily declined since the 1970s, the incidence of hunger-poverty is reported to have increased. The studies states that this divergence is due to two reasons. First, the normative calorie norm that has been used to calculate hunger-poverty has remained the same since the 1970s (2,100calories per person per day). Second, urban areas – comprising both small towns with a population of 5,000 person's population and large cities with over ten million populations – are treated as a single entity by all the empirical studies. Dubey et al. (2001) have reported that the incidence of poverty in metropolitan cities is only about one-half of that in the smaller towns.

Mishra and Lyngskor (2005) studied poverty, dietary imbalance and sickness among casual labourer in Shillong, India. Their findings show that average per capita (per month) income and consumption expenditure are Rs. 516.61 and Rs. 392.13 respectively. The poverty line as estimated by them in urban areas of Meghalaya came out to Rs. 395.6. From these they showed that 38.4 percent of the total populations surveyed were under poverty. The average energy intake among the Below Poverty Line (BPL) households is 1307.66 calories per person per day. The result of their finding regarding sickness was that, 77.78 percent are in the poverty. Thus the poverty line has been changing over the time and from scholars to scholars.

Statement of the Problem

Poverty, as the phenomenon accompanying to all economic systems, existed in all times. That 1.3 billion people, i.e. one in every five person on earth, survive on less than $1 a day and 2.8 billion people in the world live on less than $2 a day,[28] this indicates that nearly half of the people in the world live in poverty. The case for public action to eradicate malnutrition and poverty is a strong one, and one that can be forcefully made using either ethical or economic arguments. But public action to reduce malnutrition and poverty is a moral imperative. However, food and nutrition are human rights enshrined in various conventions and most recently the 1989 convention on the rights of the child. Thus, the government has a duty to ensure that these dimensions of human well being are realized.[29] Following the convention, many

Governments and nations have followed eradication of malnutrition and poverty as their main development objectives. The declaration of the 1st Millennium Development Goal of the World Bank has underlined the importance of eradication of poverty. The Millennium Development Goal call for reducing the proportion of people living on less than $1 a day to half the 1990 level by 2015 – from 27.9 percent of all people in low and middle income economies to 14.0 percent. The Goal also calls for halving the proportion of people who suffer from hunger between 1990 and 2015.[30] Thus, eradication of poverty is taking the centre stage in all nations' development agenda.

It was only in the twentieth century that poverty and the poor have come to be a matter of concern and obligation in India. After a long neglect of the poor during the British rule, the measure adopted after independence signify the recognition of poverty and the social responsibility for alleviating and reducing it. Thus, in India, poverty was with us during the colonial period and is still prevalent even after 50 years of independence. One of the objectives of the planning is to reduce inequalities of income and wealth and to set up a socialist society based on equality and justice and absence of exploitation.[31] But despite all the pious sentiment for the weaker sections the number of the poor continued to swell in the country. The *Garibi Hatao* (remove poverty) slogan raised during the parliamentary elections of 1971 brought a sharp focus on the problems of poverty. Thus, in the fifth plan, direct attack on the problem of unemployment and under-employment were launched to end poverty.[32] There is no doubt that as a result of intensification of the poverty eradication programmes, such as. IRDP, JRY, etc., by the successive government, the poverty level has started to move in the down ward direction. However, the successive round of NSSO shows a chronic prevalence of poverty in the country with some signs of slowing down. At the national level, the 56th round of the National Sample Survey Organisation's (NSSO) household survey indicates that poverty level is 26.10 % in 1999-2000. This poverty numbers are derived from sample surveys carried out by the NSSO on consumer expenditure.

Nagaland, the 16th state of Indian Union is no exception to other state when it comes to poverty. Nagaland, even after more than four decades of statehood, has 32.67 percentages of people living below poverty line during 1999-00. Moreover, the phenomenon of poverty is dominant in the rural areas with 40.04% of people living below the poverty line as compared to 7.47% of the poor in urban areas. However, it is to be noted here that the poverty ratio of Assam is being used to measure the extent of poverty of Nagaland[33] that is not appropriate. Thus, estimating the extent and depth of poverty in Nagaland based on its own norms becomes vital. In Nagaland, no individual or government agencies have brought out the nutritional norms and poverty line for the state except the one provided by NSSO. It is for these reasons the study on Nutrition and Poverty in Nagaland was done to fill the lacuna in this area.

Area and Period of Study

Nagaland has an area of 16,597 sq.km with a population of 19,88,636, out of which 82.26% live in the rural areas. It has eleven districts at present, *viz.* Dimapur, Kiphire, Kohima, Longleng, Mokokchung, Mon, Peren, Phek, Tuensang, Wokha and Zunheboto. The state is mostly inhabited by tribal population having similar socio-economic conditions. Now considering all the common features of development, habits, and social life of the rural people in the state, a study of Wokha district has been taken as a representative study for the rest of the rural areas of Nagaland. Wokha district has an area of 1,628 sq.km inhibited by Lotha tribe with a population of 1, 61,098 that constitutes 8.1% of the state's population. Out of the total population, 76.61% consist of rural population and the urban population consists of 23.48%. The literacy rate is 73.92%.[34] The district is divided into three geographical ranges, *viz,* Lower range, Middle range and Upper range showing a total of 128 villages. Taking into account the common socio-economic features of the district, four villages were selected under the present study. As a representative of their respective ranges, one village from the lower, two villages from the middle and one village from the upper range were selected.

Two villages were selected from the middle ranges because this range is having the maximum number (60) of the villages while upper range has 30 villages and the lower range 38 villages. The study estimated the average calorie requirement through nutritional intake and the monthly per capita expenditure (MPCE) of the people in the villages during the period 2005-06.

Objectives

The study has been conducted with the following objectives.

1. To study the level of socio-economic development in the study area.
2. To assess the average calorie norms per day and derive the poverty line for the sample population and compare it with national calorie norms/poverty line and state calorie norms/ poverty line given by NSSO 2004-05.
3. To estimate the average calorie requirement and the inter-variation in the calorie intake for the cross section of the population (different income, age and gender, village-wise, range-wise, sex-wise and occupation-wise head of the household).
4. To assess the relationship between the calorie intake and the family size, income and MPCE.
5. To measure the extent of poverty and inequalities in calorie intake and MPCE.
6. To assess the impact of governments poverty alleviation programmes undertaken in the village on the sample population.
7. To suggest policy options for implementing poverty alleviation programme.

Hypotheses of the Study

In order to achieve the objective stated above, the study tested the following hypotheses:

a. Low-income groups are vulnerable to poor diet and nutrition and thus, MPCE is positively correlated with higher incidence of poverty.

b. Higher the size of the household, lower is the per capita calorie intake.

c. Higher the size of the household, lower is the monthly per capita expenditure.

d. Higher the extent of inequalities (measured by Gini coefficient) in income and calorie distribution, higher is the proportion of poor (measured using the sample norms/poverty line) in the society.

Methodology

1. The concepts and definitions used while collecting and analyzing data are given below.

(i) *Household:* A group of person's normally living together and taking food from a common kitchen constitutes a household. The word "normally" means that temporary visitors are excluded but temporary stay-away are included.

(ii) *Household size:* The size of a household is the total number of persons in the household.

(iii) *Household consumption expenditure*: The expenditure incurred by a household on domestic consumption during the reference period is the household's consumption expenditure. Household consumption expenditure is the total of the monetary values of consumption of various groups of items, namely food.

It is pertinent to mention here that the consumer expenditure of a household on food items relates to the actual consumption by the members of the household and also by the guests during ceremonies or otherwise. To avoid double counting, transfer payments like charity, loan advance, etc. made by the household are not considered as consumption for items, since transfer receipts of these items have been taken into account.

(iii) *Value of consumption*: Consumption out of purchase is evaluated at the purchase price. Consumption out of home produce is evaluated at ex farm or ex factory rate. Value of consumption out of gifts, loans, free collections, and goods received in exchange of goods and services is imputed at the rate of average local retail prices prevailing during the reference period.

(iv) *Monthly per capita consumer expenditure (MPCE)*: For a household, this is the total consumer expenditure over all items divided by its size and expressed on a per month (30 days) basis. A person's MPCE is understood as that of the household to which he or she belongs.

(v) *Reference periods*: The reference periods used for collection of consumption data on items are for the last 30 days and 365 days. The data of households expenditure on foods, pan, tobacco and intoxicants, fuel and light, miscellaneous goods and services, including non-institutional medical care, rents and, taxes, cereals, egg, fish and meat, fruits (fresh and dry), conveyance etc. are collected over the last 30 days prior to the survey. The household expenditures data on clothing, footwear, education, medical care and durable goods which are not frequent, are collected over the last 365 days prior to the survey, thereafter, the total expenditure is divided by 12 months so as to arrive at monthly average expenditure.

2 Sources of Data

(i) Primary and Secondary data

The study is based on both primary and secondary data. The secondary data have been collected from the published as well as unpublished sources such as, government official records, statistical hand books, census reports, journals, newspapers, etc. While the primary data were collected through sample survey using direct personal interviews and questionnaire methods.

3. Sample design

The primary data were collected using stratified random sampling method during 2005-06. The villages were stratified according to well defined geographical ranges in the first stage. From the three ranges of Wokha districts, four villages were selected as sample villages representing their respective ranges. Accordingly upper range is represented by Longsa, middle range by Yunchuchu and Sunglup villages and the lower range by Bhandari village.

Secondly, a total of 99 households were selected as sample household that fairly represent the universe of the study. The village-wise households samples are as follows, 68 households from Longsa that constituted 10% of the total household in the village, 9 households from Yunchuchu village that constituted 10.59% of the total households in the village, 12 households from Sunglup that constituted 10.17% of the total households in the village and 10 households from Bhandari that constituted 10.42% of the total households in the village. Thus, the sample survey covered 10% of the households from each sample villages. This includes 393 individuals that encompass 5.39% of the total sample village population. The village-wise sample populations covered by the survey are as follows, Longsa with 259 persons accounting for 4.93% of the total village population, Yunchuchu, Sunglup and Bhandari villages with 42, 38, and 54 persons respectively accounting for 4.97%, 4.32% and 17.36% of their respective village population.

Further, the data on consumption of food were collected at the individual level from the sample population. Then, the collected data were converted into calories using the nutritional chart of the NSSO report 513 (61/1.0/6). Moreover, the data of expenditure on food and non-food items and their monthly income were collected at household level from the sample household.

Lastly, the information on the household's access to government poverty alleviation programmes was also collected.

4. Data Analysis

The collected data were analysed at the households and individual levels using the following statistical tools, such as, *(i)* *Mean:* It is obtained by dividing the sum of values of observations by the number of observations. It is easy to compute and understand. The formula is given below:

$$x = \frac{\Sigma x}{N}$$

x is the Arithmetic means, Σx is the sum of the variables and N is the number of observation.

(ii) *Standard Deviation:* Standard deviation is also known as root mean square deviation for reason that it is the square root of the mean of the squared deviation from the arithmetic mean. The greater the standard deviation, the greater will be the magnitude of the deviations of the values from their mean. A smaller standard deviation means a high degree of uniformity of the observation as well as homogeneity of a series; a large standard deviation means just the opposite. It is represented by sigma and is given below:

$\sigma = \sqrt{\Sigma fd^2/N - (\text{“}fd/N)^2} \times i$

Where i is the class interval.

(iii) *Coefficient of Variation:* The relative measure of dispersion is known as coefficient of variation. The series for which the coefficient of variation is greater is said to be more variable or less consistent. On the other hand, the series for which coefficient of variation is less is said to be less variable or more consistent. It is given as,

$C.V = \sigma/\text{Mean} \times 100$

(iv) *Variance:* The variance of a set of number is the square of the standard deviation. It is given as,

$\text{Variance} = \sigma^2$

(vi) *Correlation:* If the change in one variable affects a change in the other variable, the variables are said to be correlated. If the variables deviate in the same direction, correlation is said to be positive. But if they constantly deviate in the

opposite directions, correlation is negative. It is useful in determining the dependency of one variable with the other. The formula is as follows;

$$R = \frac{N\Sigma dxdy - \Sigma dx\Sigma dy}{\sqrt{N\Sigma dx^2 - (\Sigma dx)^2}\sqrt{N\Sigma dy^2 - (\Sigma dy)^2}}$$

(vii) *Probable Error:* The probable error of the coefficient of correlation helps in interpreting its value. With the help probable error it is possible to determine the reliability of the value of the coefficient in so far as it depends on the conditions of random sampling. The probable error of the coefficient of correlation is obtained as follows;

$$P.E._r = 0.6745 \quad \frac{1-r^2}{\sqrt{N}}$$

Where r is the coefficient of correlation and N is the number of pairs of observation.

a) If r is less than the probable error, there is no evidence of correlation, i.e., the value of r is not significant.

b) If r is more than six times the probable error, the coefficient of correlation is practically certain, i.e., the value of r is significant.

(viii) *Regression:* Regression analysis is a mathematical measure of the average relationship between two or more variables in terms of the original units of data. In regression there are two variables. The variable whose value influenced or is to be predicted is called dependent variable and the variable which influences the values or is used for prediction is called independent variable. Regression equation of y on x is as

$$y = a + bx$$

Where a is the intercept, y is the dependent variables, x is the independent variables and b is the regression coefficient.

$$b_{yx} = \frac{N\Sigma YX - (\Sigma Y)(\Sigma X)}{N\Sigma x^2 - (\Sigma X)^2}$$

(ix) *Standard Error Estimates:* The measure which indicates how precise the prediction of y is, based on x or conversely or how inaccurate the prediction might be is called the standard error of estimates. The standard error of regression of y values from y_c is given as

$$S_{yx} = \frac{\sqrt{\Sigma Y^2 - a\Sigma Y - b\Sigma XY}}{N}$$

The smaller the value of standard error estimates, the closer will be the dots to the regression line and the better the estimates based on the equation of this line. If the standard error of the estimates is zero, then there is no variation about the line and the correlation will be perfect.

(x) *Measures of Poverty and Inequality:* In order to measure poverty and the extent of relative inequality in the area under study, the following measures have been applied.

(a) *Head Count Ratio (H):* This measures gives the proportion of the total population deemed to be poor (i,e, those below poverty line). Let Z be the poverty line and Y be the income/calorie intake of the person with income/calorie intake arranged in ascending order so that $Y_i \leq Y_{i+1}$ for all I, let 'n' denote the total number of people in the community and 'q' the number of people below poverty line.

The Head Count Ratio (H) is then

$$H = q/n$$

But Sen observed in 1976 that head count Ratio (H) is very crude index. This index is highly insensitive to the extent of the aggregate short fall of the income from the poverty line as well as to the distribution of income amongst the poor.

(b) *Poverty Gap Index (PG):* This is an indicator which measures the depth of poverty. It depends on the distance of the poor below the poverty line (Z) the Poverty Gap. Where Z = Poverty line, Yi = income/calorie intake of the poorest poor.

$$PG = \frac{1}{n}\sum_{i+1}^{q}(Z - Y_i / Z)$$

PG could also be defined as the mean proportionate poverty gap across the whole population (zero gaps for non-poor). PG also has an interpretation as an indicator of the potential for eliminating poverty by targeting transfer to poor. The minimum cost of eliminating poverty using targeted transfers simply the sum of all the poverty in a population. One drawback of the poverty gap measure is that it ignores the number actually in poverty.[35]

(c) *Lorenz Curve:* Income/calorie intake inequalities in different groups have been examined with the help of Lorenz Curve. The Lorenz Curve shows the percentage of income/calorie intake received by X percent of population, X varying from 0 to 100. The advantage of Lorenz Curve comparison is that we can say something about the comparative levels of social welfare without specifying anything very particular about the exact welfare function. The degree to which a line Lorenz Curve deviates from the line of equal distribution is a measure of inequality of distributions of incomes/calorie intake. The further the Curve moves away from this line the greater is the inequality. The degree of this inequality at any stage is indicated by the distance from the equal distribution line. But sometimes distribution does not have this property. Thus in the study on the distribution of income/calorie intake, references is frequently made to the Gini-Co-efficient measure.

(d) *Gini-Coefficient (G_p):* Gini-Coefficient is used to attach some absolute measures to the degree of inequality or gives some idea whether the inequality is large or small. Gini-Coefficient is not purely statistical and it embodies implicit judgment about the weight to be attached to inequality at different points on the income scale. This co-efficient may be interpreted in two ways. First, it may be seen geometrically in terms of Lorenz Curve.

$$\text{Gini Coefficient} = \frac{\text{Area between Lorenz Curve and Diagonal}}{\text{Total Area under Diagonal}}$$

The co-efficient may be seen to range from zero when income/calorie intake is equal (The Lorenz Curve follows the Diagonal) to one and at the other extreme (The Lorenz Curve have > shape). Secondly, it may be computed mathematically using Rao's definition[36] as follows. Area between Lorenz Curve and Diagonal (G) is given by:

$$G = \sum_{i=1}^{n-1} (F_i Q_{i+1} - F_{i+1} Q_i)$$

(e) *Sen Index (P):* The measure of poverty proposed by Sen incorporates the number of poor, the income/calorie shortfall of the calorie norms/poverty line and the transfer of income/calorie from the poor to the very poor. The Index is given as,

$P = q/n \,.\, 1/z\,[z - v + q/q+1\, vG_p]$

n = Total population.

q = Total number of poor.

z = Calorie norms/income requirement.

v = Mean calorie intake/income of the poor people.

yi = Calorie intake/income of a poor person.

Where z is the poverty line and v is the mean income of the poor. The index P lies in between 0 to 1. It assumes the value 0 when everyone's income/calorie intake is above the calorie norms/poverty line z and the value 1 when everyone has zero income/calorie intake implying everyone is below the calorie norms/poverty line. One serious limitation of Sen Index is it is not decomposable.

The poverty index suggested by Foster, Greer and Thorbecke takes care of this problem.

(f) *Foster, Greer and Thorbecke Measure (P^F):* This measure is decomposable and takes care of the limitation of Sen Index. This is an indicator which is used to measure how income/calorie intake is distributed below the calorie intake/poverty line and takes into account the intensity and severity of poverty. It is given by:

$$(P^F) = \frac{1}{n} \sum_{i+1}^{q} (Z - Y_i / Z)^2$$

This could be defined as the mean squared proportionate poverty gaps (Ravallion, M. 1992).

NOTES

1. Galbriath, J. K. (1979), *The Nature of Mass Poverty*, Harvard University press, Cambridge, pp.20-21.
2. Haq, M. U. (1978), *The Poverty Curtain: Choices for the Third World*, Oxford University press, New York, p.XV.
3. Prasad, K. N. (1980), *Problem of Economic Development in the Third World: With Special References to India*, New Delhi, Sterling Publishers, p.102.
4. Joshi, P. C. (1985), "Poverty Amelioration Perspective", *IASSI Quarterly News Letter*, June 1985, p. 14.
5. WHO (2004); "Poverty, disability and community based Rehabilitation (CBR) Programme". UN ESCAP/CDPF Field Study cum Regional *Workshop on Poverty Alleviation Among Persons with Disabilities*, Lanzhou, China, Oct. 2004. Online [available] at www.DAR@who.int. p. 4.
6. Gross, R. (1997), "Nutrition and the Alleviation of Absolute Poverty in Communities: Concepts and Measurement", *Symposium on "Nutrition and Poverty" with a special emphasis on South Asia*, 24th Session of the ACC/, Nepal on 17-21 March 1997, p. 2.
7. Ahuja, R. (1992), *Social Problems in India*, Rawat Publication, New Delhi, p. 30.
8. Dubey, A. and Sarma, A. (2000), "Poverty Measurement and Mobility Issues", *Discussion Paper*, Center for Development and Community Consulting. GOI, p. 3.

9. Townsend P. (1979), "Poverty in the United Kingdom", p.31, Online [available] at *www.archiveshub.ac.uk*.
10. Lipton, M. and Ravillion, M. (1995), "Poverty and Policy", in J. Berhman and T. N. Srinivasan (ed.), *Handbook of Development Economics*: Vol. III, Elsevier Science, p 2551 – 52.
11. Horowitz, A. (1997); "Poverty and Nutrition in South Asia", The 24th Session of ACC/SCN, Kathmandu, Nepal on 17-21 March 1997, Symposium on *Nutrition and Poverty; with a special emphasis on South Asia.* p.5.
12. *Webster's New Collegiate Dictionary*, 1956: G. & C. Merriam Co., Publishers, Springfield, MA. p 403.
13. Hunger Task Force, 2003: *Halving Hunger by 2015: A Framework for Action,* Interim Report, Millennium Project, UNDP, New York. p. 33.
14. Dasgupta, P., 1993: *An inquiry into well-being and destitution,* Oxford University Press, Oxford. p 3.
15. Friel, S. (2004), "Nutrition, Poverty and Health", *National Conference*, North West Ireland, p.4. Online [available] at www.cpa.ie/downloads/publication/conference.
16. Islam, R. (1997), "Poverty and Its Effect on Nutrition: Some Question Based on the Asian Experience", p.2. Online [available] at *www.unsystem.org*.
17. Prabhu, S. (2001), "World Development; Destitution and the Poverty of its Politics", p.7, Online [available] at *www.linkinghub.elsevier.com*.
18. Becker, H. (1996), *Social Problems: A Modern Approach,* John Willy and Son Inc., New York, p.436.
19. Government of India (1993), *Report of the Expert Group on Estimation of Proportion and Number o fPoor*, Planning Commission, p. 3.
20. Government of India (2001), "Nurtitional Intake in India", *NSS Report 471*, 1999-00, p. 1.
21. Sen, P. (2005), "Of Calories and Things: Reflection on Nutritional Norms, Poverty Lines and Consumption Behaviour in India", *Economic and Political Weekly*, Vol XL. No.43, 2005, p. 4611.
22. Ojha, P. D. (1970); "A Configuration of Indian Poverty: Inequality and Level of Lining", *RBI Bulletin,* January 1970.
23. Dandekar, V. M. and Rath, N. (1971); "Poverty in India, Indian School of Political Economy," p 8-18 (Reprinted from *Economic and Political Weekly*, Bombay, Volume VI, Nos 1 and 2, January 2 and 9, 1971).

24. Bardhan, P. K (1973). "On the Incidence of Poverty in Rural India", *Annual Number*, February 1973, pp. 245-46.

25. Minhas, B.S. (1970); "Rural Poverty, Land Redistribution and Development Strategy: Facts and Policy", *Indian Economic Review*, April 1970, Reproduced in Minhas, *Planning and the Poor*, S. Chand and Co., 1978, Chapter II.

26. Datt, G. and Ravallion, M. (1989), "Regional Disparities, Targeting and Poverty in India", *Working Paper No. 375*, World Bank, p.37.

27. Dubey, A.and Gangopadhyay, S. (1998), "Counting the poor: Where are the poor in India", *Sarvekshana: Analytical Report*, Department of Statistics, Goveernment of India, No. 1, 1998, p. 2.

28. *Ibid* 4.

29 Haddad, L. (2002), "Nutrition and Poverty", *In Nutrition: A foundation for Development*, Geneva: ACC/SCN. p 1.

30. World Bank (2000), "Millineium Goal for World Development" On-line available at *www.ddp-ext.worldbank.org/ext/MGD/home.do.*

31. Datt R and Sundharam K.P.M, *Indian Economy*, 6th edition, 2002, p.155.

32. GOI (1972), *Towards an Approach to the Fifth Plan*, Planning Commission, New Delhi, p. 7.

33. Kapila, U. (2007), *Indian Economy; Issues in Development and Planning and Sectoral Aspects*, 5th edition, Academic Foundation, New Delhi. pp. 213-4.

34. Government of Nagaland (2004), *Statistical Handbook of Nagaland 2004*, Directorate of Economics and Statistics Nagaland, Kohima.

35. Anand, S. (2002), "The Definition and Measurement of Poverty", In Subramanian S (ed) 2002, *Measurement of Inequality and Poverty*, p. 250.

36. *Ibid.*

2

Socioeconomic Conditions of the Study Area

India is a land of villages and more than 70 per cent of its population lives in the countryside. Village is the heart and soul of Indian economy. Therefore, it is imperative to look into the socio-economic condition of the rural areas as that would give a major view on country's economic progress and development. In Nagaland, there are 1,317 villages, out of which 1, 278 are inhabited. Most of the thousand odd villages' stands at 1 to 2000 metres high as it is very typical of the Naga's to build their houses on the hill top and at higher elevation. Therefore, it is imperative to look into the socio-economic condition of the rural areas as that would give significant glue to existence of poverty in the state. Modern economist also views development as both physical and a state of mind, in which, society has, through some combination of economic, social and institutional process, secured the means for obtaining a better life that fulfills the objectives of (i) increase in availability of basic life subsistence like food, shelter, health and protection, (ii) raise in the level of living through higher income, job opportunities and better education and (iii) expand the range of economic and social choices available to individuals by freeing them from servitude and dependence.[1] Thus, this chapter seeks to examine the extent of socio-economic development in Nagaland in general and Wokha district in particular using some indicators. The selected indicators are as follows, (i) demographic dynamics, (ii) sectoral employment and its contribution to NSDP, (iii) physical infrastructure – transport and communications, electricity and banking, (iv) social services, housing, health, education, water supply and sanitation and (v) co-operatives.

Historical Background and Physical Feature of the State and District

Nagaland, the 16th state of Indian Union, was inaugurated on 1st of December 1963. The state lies between 25°60′ and 27°40′ latitude north of equator and between the longitudinal lines 93°20′ E and 95°15′ E having an area of 16,579 sq.kms. The state is bounded by Assam in the North and West, by Myanmar and Arunachal Pradesh in the East and Manipur in the South and runs more or less parallel to the left bank of Brahmaputra. The topography is of the state is of a hilly ranges, which break into a wide chaos of spurs and ridges. The altitude varies between 194 metres and 3048 metres. The highest peak in the state is Mt. Saramati, which is 3, 840 metres above the sea level. The State has eleven districts at present, *viz.*, Dimapur, Kiphire, Kohima, Longleng, Mokokchung, Mon, Peren, Phek, Tuensang, Wokha and Zunheboto. There are 1,317 villages in the state, out of which 1,278 are inhabited. The state is almost entirely inhabited by tribals. There are many separate tribes and sub-tribes amongst the Nagas, with their own distinctive language and cultural features, viz, Angamis, Aos, Lothas, Semas, Sangtams, Konyaks etc (GON, 2004).

The focus area of the present study is Wokha district of Nagaland. Wokha district is bounded by Mokokchung and Assam in the North, Assam in the West, Kohima in the south and Zunheboto in the east. In the year 1876, the British Government occupied Wokha as the district headquarters of the Naga Hills under Assam. In 1878, the headquarters was shifted to Kohima and thereafter Wokha became a sub-division. Later in 1889, the sub-division was again shifted to Mokokchung. Only in the year 1957, when Mokokchung became a separate district, Wokha was restored to the status of sub-division under the district. In the year 1973 that Wokha was granted a full-fledged district.[2] Wokha district has an area of 1,628 sq. km (GON, 2001) inhabited by Lotha tribe. The district is divided into three ranges, viz, Upper, Middle and Lower range. It is equidistant at 80 km both from Kohima as well as Mokokchung. Wokha literally means counting of votes in Lotha dialect. Wokha district enjoys a moderate and pleasant climate. The topography of the district is more or less similar with that of other district in the state, having hilly ranges and ridges dissected by seasonal streams. The altitude ranges from 303.3 metres to 1313.67 metres above the sea level. The highest elevation of the district is Mt. Tiyi with the height of 1970 metre above the sea level. The annual rainfall varies from 200 cms to 250 cms. Important rivers of the district are Doyang, Chubi, Nzhu and Nruk.. The district has a total of 129 villages, out of which 128 villages were inhabited and 1 inhabited (GON, 2004). An interesting and similar feature of these villages is that, every village's rear animals, cultivate rice and vegetables and collect wild vegetables for their consumption.

Demographic Dynamics of the State and District

Population plays an important role in affecting the income and consumption levels and thereby the living standard of any society.[3] In Nagaland, the total population enumerated in 2001 census was 19, 88,636. Out of this, 10, 41,686 are males and 9, 46,950 are females,[4] giving a sex ratio of 909 per thousand male that is lower than the national ratio of 933. The density of population is 120 per sq. km., which is lower than the national level of 324 persons per sq. km. These highlight the difference in the magnitude of the burden that land is being called upon to carry. In this sense, the state is not as highly populated and over burden as compared with the country as a whole. However, in view of the state's hilly topographical feature and the slow pace of economic development, the rapid rate of population growth of 69.44% during the last decade and the total fertility rate of 3.77 in 1998,[5] which rates are the highest in the country, are matters of concern. Further, there has been a progressive increase in the number of urban population from 2,08,162.87 in 1991 to 3,52, 784.03 in 2001, yet the proportion of people residing in urban area was increased only marginally from 17.21% to 17.74% during the same period. This is lower than the national average of 27.78%. Thus, Nagaland continues to be predominantly rural accounting for 16, 35, 815 (82.26%) of the total population. Among the districts, at one extreme, Tuensang has a population of 4.14 lakh that account for 20.86% of the state population and on the other extreme, Phek has only 1.48 lakh that accounts for 7.45% of the state population. The average household size is 6.1 persons (census 2001). The tribal constitutes 89.1% of Nagaland population.

In 2001, out of the State's total population, 1, 61,098 persons live in Wokha district that consist of 8.10% of the total population. The proportion of rural population in the district is, 1,23,402 accounting for 76.61% of the total district population, which is lower than the State average. The proportion of urban population is 37,696 accounting for 23.39% of the total population, which is higher than the state average. The sex ratio is 927, which is also higher than the state's ratio. But there is a significant difference between rural and urban areas in this respect. In rural areas sex ratio is 952 as compared to 843 in the urban areas. It may be noted that Wokha district has the highest decennial population growth rate of 1991-2001 (95.01%) in the state as well as at the national level. However, the density of population is 99.03 persons per sq.km only, which is lower than the state as well as the country's averages. The average household size is higher than the state average with 6.23 persons.

Sectoral Employment and its Contribution to NSDP of the State and District

In Nagaland, workers constitute 42.74% of its total population. Naga society is predominantly agrarian where 68.03% of the working force are engaged in agriculture and allied activities. In absolute terms, out of the total 8,49,983 workers, 5,44,432 are cultivators and 33,852 are agricultural labourers that account for 64.05% and 3.98% respectively. Household industrial sector employs 18,072 workers and 2,53,625 are other worker that constitutes 2.13% and 29.84% respectively of the total workers. Comparatively, Wokha district has a total workforce of 56,453 giving a lower percentage (35.04%). The district shares a similar pattern of sectoral distribution of workers to that of the state. The total workforce engaged in agricultural sector as cultivator and agricultural labour adds up to 37,295 workers that accounts for 66.06% of the total workforce in the district. Whereas, 1,435 workers are engaged in household industries and 17,723 are engaged in other services/works, accounting for 2.54% and 31.39% respectively of the total workforce.

The gender-wise distribution of workers in the state shows that male dominates the employment sector with 57.35%. The share of female employment in agricultural sector and household industries together accounted for 50.32% whereas male's share is closer to female with 49.68%. The share of male worker in other sector is 75.50% of the sector work force. Comparatively, the gender-wise distribution of workers in Wokha district reveals that male dominates the employment sector with 55.66%. However, sector-wise data reveals that agricultural and household industries are dominated by female workers with 54.92% and 66.06% respectively. It is only in other work where male shares a higher with 79.09% of the total sector workforce.

The unemployment scenarios in Nagaland, as on March 2000, showed that 35,000 were job seekers who had registered at the state employment exchange. Out of this total, 3, 000 were graduates and post graduates, 13,000 were matriculates and 14,000 were under matriculates.[6] This brings out the fact that majority of (91.43%) unemployed persons in the state are not even graduates, indicating the quality of the workforce available. However, these statistics do not fully represent the extent of unemployment, as large number of unemployed persons does not get registered.

The sectoral contribution to NSDP for the period 1997-98 to 2001-02 at 1993-94 prices in the state reveals that the share of primary sector has increased from 26.21 percent to 36.68 percent, while the share of secondary sector and tertiary sector have declined from 20.04 percent to 10.25 and from 53.75 percent to 53.07 percent respectively during the same period (GON, 2004). These facts point that the primary sector is gaining importance over the other sector in the state NSDP. However, the share of tertiary sector in NSDP is still higher than the other sectors even though it has declined marginally over the years.

Physical Infrastructure of the State and District

It is concern with the needs of facilities for production sector like agriculture, industry, trade, etc. which include services such as power, transport, telecommunication, etc.[7]

(a) Transport and communication: One of the important features of development is better infrastructure in transport and communication. It is the basic infrastructure needed for generating economic activities for the land-locked hilly state like Nagaland. Thus, an all-weather road linking the scattered villages is the pre-requisite for development of potential areas. The total length of road in the state as on 2002-03 is 13, 368.45 kms, out of which 6,225.62 kms are surfaced and are all weather roads, while 7,142.83 kms are unsurfaced. National highway accounts for 248 kms, while village roads account for 5,150 Kms. The surfaced roads or all weather roads in the villages, account for 2,129 kms (GON, 2004). In Nagaland only 23.61% of the villages (311) are having pucca road link, 56.95% of the villages (750) are connected with Kutcha road (VLDI, 2002) while 19.44% of the villages (256) do not have a link road. Moreover, the state is connected with one airport and railway station both located at Dimapur. Comparatively, the national highway 61 passes through Wokha district covering only 37 km, which constituted 14.92% of the total national highway in the state. Of the total villages in the district, only 22 villages (17.05%) are linked by pucca road and 82 villages are having only kutcha road. The rest 25 villages of the district do not have any link road (VLDI, 2002). Thus, 80.62% of the total villages in the district have a road link, which is slightly higher than the state average of 80.56%. Since there are many villages, which are not covered by all weather roads, it clearly depicts the extent of deprivation of the villagers from all aspects of

socio-economic development in general and ready access of farmer's products to the markets in particular. Moreover, the district is neither connected by railway nor airport.

In the area of communication, the state is not lagging behind. The number of post office including one head office serving the entire population of the State during 2004 is 328. Out of the total post offices, branch post office account for 284, while the number of sub-post office in the state is 43. The telephone connection in the state as on 2001-02 is 38,597 (GON, 2004). In comparison, the district has 2 sub-post offices, that accounts for 4.65% of the state sub-post offices and 20 branch offices accounting for 7.04% of the state total branch offices, giving us a total of 22 offices, i.e, 6.71% of the post offices in the state during 2004. There were 963 Households with telephone connections in the district accounting for 2.5% of the state telephone connection during 2001-02, one of the lowest among the districts in Nagaland (GON, 2004).

(b) Electricity: The most important factor which can act as a stimulant for economic growth of a country is that of energy. There is a direct correlation between the degree of economic growth and the size of per capita energy consumption. Among the various sources of energy, Nagaland has great potential in Hydro-electric power. Non-conventional source of energy like solar, wind and tidal power have been scarcely used. The installed capacity of Hydro-electric power in the state as on 2002-03 is 28.50 MKWH. Whereas, the generation of power in the state during the same period was 8.63 MKWH and the energy imported was 271.41 MKWH. The consumption of energy during the same period was 278.88 MKWH (GON, 2004). Thus, it implies that only 3% of the total energy requirement in the state is met by its own generation, the rest of 97% is imported from other state. Out of the total 1, 278 inhabited villages, 1, 200 villages have been electrified as on 2001-02 (GON, 2004). Thus, 93.89% of the total inhabited villages have been electrified so far. The revenue generated from the sale of power as on 2002-03 stands at Rs. 2085.90 lakhs.

Out of the total electrified villages in Nagaland Wokha district account for 10% of the total villages. Further, out of the total of

128 inhibited villages in the district, 107 were electrified in 1991. The number has increased to 120 by 2001-01 (GON, 2004). Thus, the figure clearly shows that 93.75% of the inhibited villages are having electricity facility, which is almost equivalent to that of the state average of 93.89%.

(c) Banking: Banks plays an important role in stimulating economic growth by strengthening agricultural, industrial and other self-employment activities. Banks are also credited for designing social banking policies and programmes, which supports vital sectors of the economy. It aims at alleviating poverty by benefiting number of farmers, artisans, professionals and self-employment. The banks that are operating in the state are the State Bank of India, Allahabad Bank, United Bank of India, United Commercial Bank, Vijaya Bank, Bank of Baroda apart from Nagaland Cooperative Bank and Rural Bank. The total number of scheduled commercial banks and their branches in the state as on 2002 is 85 (Economic Survey of Nagaland, 2001-02). Thus, there are 85 banks serving the entire population giving us a ratio of 1: 23,395.71 (i.e. one bank is serving a total population of 23,396). Dimapur district has the highest number with 22 banks, while Mon district has the lowest with 5 banks. The total deposits of these banks as on June 2002 stood at Rs. 93,490 lakh and credit at Rs. 13,073 lakh. Thus, the credit-deposit ratio of the state is 1: 7.15.

Out of the total banks and branches in the state, only 6 banks, viz, 4 SBI, 1 Nagaland Rural Bank and 1 State Co-operative Bank are located in Wokha district (as on June 2002). This account for 7.06% of the total banks in the state, serving a total population of 1,61,098 (Economic Survey of Nagaland, 2001-02). This gives bank - population ratio of 1: 26, 850, which is below the state ratio. The total deposit in these banks is Rs. 2, 666 lakhs and the total credit is Rs. 496 lakhs as on June 2002 (Economic Survey of Nagaland, 2001-02). This gives the credit-deposit ratio of the district as 1: 5.38, which is higher than the state ratio. As far as rural area is concern, only 1 village has the banking facilities as on 1991 (VLDI, 2002). From the above figure, it clearly indicates that there is an urgent need to increase the number of banks and their branches in the district extending its facilities to rural villages.

Social Infrastructure of the State and District

It is concerned with facilities that enhance human welfare, freedom from ignorance, diseases and fear and are collectively termed as social infrastructure such as, education, health care, water and sanitation services.[8]

(a) Education: Education is important not only for creating a means to enhance human capital, productivity and hence the compensation of labour. But it is equally important for enabling the process of acquisition, assimilation and communication of information and knowledge, all of which augments a person's quality of life. Thus, education has a great impact in developing the socio-economic status of the people. The literacy rate in the state is 67.11% (GON, 2004) that is above the national level. The male literacy rate in the state is 71.2% and female literacy rate in the state is 61.5%. One of the determinants of literacy is the existence of educational institutions. There are 2,421 educational institutions in Nagaland as on 2003-04. These institutions include primary to higher secondary schools as well as colleges and University in the state. Out of 2,421 institutions, 1,737 (71.75%) are government owned institutes and 684 (28.25%) are private owned institutions. The total number of enrollment in the institutions as on 2003-04 was 4,57,644. Out of this total, male enrollment constitutes 2,39,355 (52.30%) and female accounts for 2,18,289 (47.70%). The total number of teachers in these institutions is 21,764, out of which male teacher accounts for 14,148 (65%) whereas female teacher accounts for 7,616 (35%). Thus, in Nagaland teacher - students' ratio is 1: 21.03 as on 2003-04 and institution - student's ratio is 1: 189.03. Moreover, institution-teacher's ratio is 1: 8.99 in the state.

The literacy rate of Wokha district is 81.28% next only to Mokokchung. Male literacy rate is 85.69% and female literacy rate is 76.46%. The total enrollment of students in institutions in the district is 54.5%. Boy's enrollment rate is 55.7% surpassing girl's enrollment rate, which stands at 53.2%. The ratio of teacher and students is 1:20, which is above the state ratio of 1:21.03 (NSHDR 2003). Out of the total villages in the district, 107 (82.95%) villages have the primary schools, 33 (25.58%) villages have middle schools and 8 (6.20%) villages have high school in 1991 census (VLDI, 2002).

(b) Health: One way of understanding the quality of life is the availability of hospitals, dispensaries, primary health centres, subsidiaries health centres, sub-centres and medical practitioners (doctors, nurses and compounders). The total numbers of hospitals, primary health centres, subsidiaries health centres and sub-centres in the state, as on 2003, is 603. The total number of beds in these hospitals and centres, as on 2002 is 2,183 (GON, 2004). The number of doctors serving the entire population, as on 2003 is 367, whereas, nurses is 1,232 and the compounders are 505. Thus the total number of medical practitioners in Nagaland, as on 2003 is 2,104. This implies that one hospital or centre is serving 3,297.91 people and one medical practitioner is serving 945.17 people. The life expectancy at birth as an indicator of health is 74.4 years, which is above the national average of 62.3 years. Infant mortality rate is 42.2 per 1000 live births as compared to the national average of 68. Similarly, under-five mortality rate per 1000 live births is 63.8 as against the national average of 96 (GON, 2004). Moreover, the state expenditure in health sector as on 1998-99 is just 5.39% of the total state expenditure (NSHRD, 2003). Thus, there is an urgent need to enhance the share of government expenditure in this sector if the state's objective is welfare one.

In the case of health sector, Wokha district has a total of 61 health institution which comprises of 1 district hospital, 3 community health centres, 8 primary health centres, 5 subsidiary health centres, 1 dispensary, 42 sub-centres and 1 S.T.D clinic as on 2003. This shows that the district accounts for 9.95% of the total hospitals and centres in the state. The total medical practitioners in the district during the same period were 170, which accounted for 8.08% of the total medical practitioners in the state. Out of this total 26 are doctors, 49 compounders and 95 nurses. Thus, it shows that one hospital or centres is serving 2,640.95 people and 1 medical practitioner is serving a total of 947.63 people, which is little higher than the state level. There are a total of 170 beds in the hospitals and health centers, which accounts for 7.79% of the total beds in the state. Out of this total, 50 beds are in the urban hospital, 30 in community health centre, 78 in primary health centre, 10 in subsidiary health centre and 2 in dispensaries (GON, 2004). The facilities of hospital, primary health centre and dispensary are available only in 49 (37.98%) villages in the district as on 1991 census (VLDI, 2002). Out of this total, only one village has hospital facilities, while 48 villages have either dispensary or subsidiary health centre during the same period, whereas 62.02% of the villages in the district were left with no health care institution.

(c) Water supply and sanitation: Availability of safe dinking water and proper sanitation forms an important component of health. Thus, the supply of potable drinking water was identified as one of the thrust areas of development in the state since such amenity contributes significantly in the maintenance of health care. The accelerated rural water supply programme is sponsored by the Ministry of Rural Development, Government of India with 100% assistance and is being implemented by Public Health Engineering Department. This programme was implemented in all the districts. Consequently the household with safe drinking water facility in Nagaland has increased from 53.37 percent in 1991 to 95 percent in 2003 (NSHRD, 2004). However, majority of the villages are only partially covered with safe drinking water. The budget allocation for the facility during 2001-02 under state plan was Rs. 3, 901 lakhs, while under centrally sponsored scheme for the same period was Rs. 1,788 lakhs.

In 1991, a total of 82 villages in Wokha district were covered partially or wholly with water supply. By 2001-01 additional 24 villages were also covered with safe drinking water (GON, 2004). Thus, the total number of villages covered wholly and partially with the availability of safe drinking water has increased to 106 villages. The result reveals that 82.17% of the villages in the district were covered with drinking water supply which is below the state level coverage of 95%.

Nagaland has a significant burden of infectious diseases that is closely linked to sanitation and water facilities. According to the Nagaland State Human Development Report 2004, only 24.8% of the households in Nagaland have flush toilets and 49.4% have pit toilets. Nearly one-fourth of the population has no sanitation facility. Although Nagaland does better than the national average of 30% in terms of availability of toilets, yet much have to be done to improve this status.

Comparatively, the district level sample survey conducted by NSHDR 2004 shows that the household having access to toilets in Wokha district is 63.38% that is above the state level of 57%. The survey also show that own toilets account for 59.84% and 3.54% account for common toilets, while open defecation accounts for 36.61%. Even though the district performance as compared to other districts of the state is better, a lot more efforts and investment needs to be done in this sector because a better housing and environment is essential for healthy living conditions of the people.

(d) Housing: Another factor affecting the health as well as the general quality of life is Housing. The sample survey done by Nagaland Human Development Report 2004 revealed that majority of the sampled households across the districts lived in semi-pucca and kutcha houses. On an average 44.14% of the houses are Kutcha in the state. The district-wise figure on type of housing shows that in Mon 78% of the houses were kutcha, Phek 55%, Kohima 50% and Tuensang 45%. Thus the causes for the high prevalence of infectious diseases are to be attributed to factors like, poor housing, sanitation and environment that surround them.

As per the survey conducted by NSHRD 2004, in Wokha district 18.90% of the total household is having a pucca house next only to Dimapur district, while 59.06% of the households are living in semi-pucca houses. The data also show that Wokha district is having the highest number of households with semi-pucca houses followed by Mokokchung with 58.33%. The rest of the households are residing in kutcha houses that accounts for 22.04%. Thus in terms of housing facilities, the district exhibit a better condition than other district in the state with 77.96% of the households being either in pucca or semi-pucca houses, followed by Mokokchung with 76.93%.

Cooperative Societies of the State and District

The ideology of co-operation is based on the principle of self-help, self-responsibility, democracy, equity and solidarity. The main objective of co-operation is propagation of co-operative education and training to members, office bearers, employees of the co-operatives societies and general masses for creating enlightened membership, improving business efficiency, developing leadership and co-operative awareness. The co-operative movement in the country traces its origin to the agriculture and allied sector, which originally evolved as a mechanism for pooling the people's meager resources with a view to providing them the advantages of the economic scales. In Nagaland element of co-operation was firmly rooted in the tribal mode of life. It continues to play a vital role in the social and economic development of the state. It has made significant progress in terms of number of societies and number of members. The state has 5306 co-operatives societies of different types in various districts out of which 167 were registered during the year 2001-02. From 634 audited societies in 2001-02, the total amount was estimated to be Rs. 4,48,149 (Economic Survey of Nagaland, 2001-02). It is expected that these societies significantly contribute in uplifting the socio-economic conditions especially in rural areas.

There are 106 co-operative societies in Wokha district as on 2001-02, accounting for 1.99% of state total co-operatives (Economic survey, 2001-02). During 2000-01 the integrated co-operative development project (ICDP) has been approved by the state government and entrust state co-operative banks for the project. The recovery of ICDP loans during 2000-02 in the district was 4.34 lakh.

Socio-economic Profile of the Sample Villages

The village organization in Nagaland is primarily based on institution of clan, which is considered as the basic unit of the society. A clan is a group of families amongst where inter-marriage is strictly prohibited. Generally, two or more such clans form a Naga village (GON, 1998). Further, a Naga village is divided into number of Khels (wards or hamlets) according to the size of the village. The unique features of each Naga village are the family, clan and community. The houses are primarily built of thatch, wood and bamboos. As society progress, one can see pucca houses in the villages too. In this section, socio-economic profile of the sample villages is highlighted. The study focused on the four villages of the district, viz, Longsa (Upper Range), Yunchuchu and Sunglup (Middle Range) and Bhandari (Lower Range).

Longsa Village: The village is situated at the upper range of Wokha Districts, 5 km away from Wokha Town (*Statistical Hand Book of Nagaland*, 2004). The village is connected with pucca road (constructed in 2005). It has 680 households with a total population of 5250; out of which 2475 are males and 2775 are females (VDB report 2002). There are 4 educational institutions in the village which comprises of 1 middle school and 3 primary schools. Out of these 2 schools are government owned and 2 are private owned. The government water supply does not cover the village. A total of 650 households in the village are electrified accounting for 92.65% of the total household in the village. The village has one dispensary with 4 workers.

Yunchuchu Village: This village is situated in the middle range of Wokha District, 43 km away from the main district headquarters (Wokha Town) and 5 km away from Sanis subdivision (*Statistical Hand Book of Nagaland*, 2004). It has a total household of 85, out of which 59 households have electricity connectivity. The village is connected with Kutcha road but not pliable during rainy season. The village solely depends on the well and streams as the source of drinking water. It has a total population of 844 out of which 378 are male and 466 are female (VDB annual report 2005). It has 1 Government primary school (till class VI) and 1 Dispensary mend by1 nurse.

Sunglup Village: This village is 45 km away from the main district headquarters (Wokha Town) situated in the middle range and the nearest suburban centre (Sanis subdivision) is 7 km away (*Statistical Hand Book of Nagaland*, 2004). The village has a total household of 118 with a total population of 880 which comprises of 420 male and 460 female (VDB annual report 2005). The village is connected by Kutcha road but not pliable during rainy season. The main sources of drinking water are streams and well. Only 36 households have been connected with electricity. The village has 2 educational institutions comprising of 1 private owned school having up to class IV and 1 government primary school having up to class VI. The village has a dispensary with one nurse who is looking after the health care need of the villagers.

Bhandari Village: Bhandari village is in the lower range of Wokha District and is located 46 km away from Wokha Town (*Statistical Hand Book of Nagaland,* 2004) and is 6 km away from Bhandari town. The village comprises of 96 households with a total population of 311, where 161 are males and 150 are females (VDB annual report 2005). The village has 1 government primary school (up to class II). Total number of households having electricity connection is 60. The main sources of drinking water are well and streams. The village is connected by kutcha road, and there is one dispensary in the village.

A comparative analysis of the data given in table number 2.1 reveals the variation among the sample villages, district and with state averages in respect to household size, sex ratio, electrification,

Table 2.1
Profile of the sample villages

Category	*Total*	*Sample Villages*			
		Longsa	*Yunchuchu*	*Sunglup*	*Bhandari*
No. of Household	979	680	85	118	96
Total Population	7285	5250	844	880	311
Male	3434	2475	378	420	161
Female	3851	2775	466	460	150
Sex ratio (per 1000 males)	1121 females	1121 females	1232 Females	1095 Females	931 Females
No. of Electrified Household	785	630	59	36	60
% of Electrified Household	80.18%	92.65%	69.41%	30.51%	62.5%
Water Supply (PHE)	0	0	0	0	0
No. of Educational institute	8	4	1	2	1
Number of Teachers	51	32	5	11	3
Number of students	485	380	35	50	20
No. of Dispensary	4	1	1	1	1
No. of Doctor	0	0	0	0	0
No. of Nurse, compounder, peon and Helper	7	4	1	1	1
Road (Pucca/ Kutcha)	1Pucca and 3 Kutcha	Pucca	Kutcha	Kutcha	Kutcha

Source: VDB unpublished official file 2005-06.
0: Not available.

water supply and sanitation, education, health and road infrastructure.

(a) Household size: The average household size for the sample villages as a whole is (7285/979) 7.44 persons, which is higher

than the district average (6.23) and state average (6.1). Inter-village analysis shows that, Yunchuchu village has the highest average household size with (844/85) 9.93 persons, followed by Longsa with (5250/680) 7.72 persons, Sunglup with (880/118) 7.46 persons and Bhandari with (311/96) 3.24 persons.

The household size at Yunchuchu village is found to be higher than the sample average, district as well as state averages by 2.49 persons, 3.7 persons and 3.83 persons respectively. Also Longsa and Sunglup villages exhibits higher average than the sample, district and the state averages. However, Bhandari village has an average that is significantly lower than the average of the sample villages, district and the state averages. The standard deviation comes to 2.79 and the variance is 7.81, revealing that there is a variation among the sample villages in the household size.

(b) Sex ratio: For the sample villages, the male population account for 3434 and female with 3851 of the total population giving a sex ratio of 1121 females per thousand males. For Longsa village, the sex ratio is 1121 females per thousand males that is equal to the sample average. For Yunchuchu village it is 1232 females per thousand males giving us higher sex ratio than the sample average. The sex ratio for Sunglup village is 1095 females per thousand males which fall below the average ratio. Bhandari village have the lowest sex ratio with 931 females per thousand males. Thus, except for Bhandari village, the sex ratio is significantly higher than the sample average. However, the sex ratio of the sample villages is higher than both the district (927) as well as the state (909) averages.

(c) Electrification: Electricity, which is one of the most essential needs of any human being, has reached the villages. Yet, only 80.18% of the total households in the sample villages are electrified. For Longsa village 92.65% of households are electrified. For Yunchuchu, Sunglup and Bhandari, electrified households are, 69.41%, 30.51% and 62.5% respectively. Moreover, except for Longsa village all the villages are below the sample average. It

clearly shows a wide-ranging variation in the availability of basic needs. The range of variation between the highest and the lowest is more than 60%. Their standard deviation is 25.65 and the variance is 657.9, showing us that there is a wide variation among the sample villages in respect of households' electrification facility.

(d) Water supply: The government's safe drinking water supply programme has not been implemented in any of the sample villages. Therefore these villages depend on natural sources like streams, well and harvested rainwater.

(e) Road: Infrastructure plays an important role in uplifting village economy. But the figure shows that except for Longsa village, all other three villages are being connected by Kutcha roads. Moreover, Longsa village has all weather road connectivity while the other three do not have all weather road connectivity.

(f) Educational institutions: The over all educational institutions in the entire study area is 8. There are 4 schools in Longsa, 2 schools in Sunglup and 1 school each in Yunchuchu and Bhandari villages. The total number of teachers in the sample villages is 51 with a total of 485 students. The teacher-student ratio is 1: 9.51 for the sample villages, which is higher than the district (1: 20) and state's (1: 21) ratio. The teacher–student ratio is highest in Sunglup with 1: 4.55, Yunchuchu with 1: 7 is next, followed by Bhandari with 1: 6.67, which is higher the average sample village ratio. However, a Longsa village has a ratio of 1: 11.88 that is lower than the sample ratio. Thus, all the sample villages have a higher ratio then the district and state's average. The institution-student ratio is 1: 60.63, which is higher state ratio of 1: 189.03. Among the sample villages, Longsa has the lowest ratio with 1: 90 that is below the sample ratio but higher than state's ratio. Sunglup and Bhandari with 1: 25 and 1: 20 respectively are at the top followed by Yunchuchu with 1: 35, are very much above the state's ratio. The institution-teacher ratio for the sample villages is 1: 6.38 that is above the state's ratio of 1: 8.99. Longsa village exhibit the lowest ratio with 1: 8 among the sample villages, which is almost the same with that of the state's ratio (1: 8.99). The rest of the sample villages: Sunglup with 1:

Table 2.2
Demographic Characteristics of the Sample Population

Category	*Total*	*Longsa*	*Yunchuchu*	*Sunglup*	*Bhandari*
Total population	393	259	42	38	54
Percentage	100	65.9	10.69	9.67	13.74
Male	172	106	18	18	30
Female	221	153	24	20	24
No of Household	99	68	9	12	10
Household size (persons)	3.97	3.81	4.67	3.17	5.4
Number of persons above 7 years of age	316	209	34	37	36
Percentage	82.95	80.69	80.95	97.37	66.67
Literate	228	149	27	21	31
Percentage	72.15	71.29	79.41	56.76	86.11
Male	120	73	10	12	25
Percentage	83.92	82.95	90.9	70.59	92.59
Female	108	76	17	9	6
Percentage	64.48	62.81	73.91	45	66.67
Illiterate	88	60	7	16	5
Percentage	27.85	28.71	20.59	43.24	13.89
Male	23	15	1	5	2
Percentage	16.08	17.05	9.1	29.41	7.41
Female	65	45	6	11	3
Percentage	35.52	37.19	26.19	55	33.33
Total work force	253	158	23	33	39
Percentage	64.38	61	54.76	86.84	72.22
Agriculturalist	152	83	15	26	28
Percentage	60.08	52.53	65.22	78.79	71.8
Male	39	13	3	10	13
Percentage	25.66	15.66	20	38.46	46.43
Female	113	70	12	16	15
Percentage	74.34	84.34	80	61.54	53.57
Non-agriculturist	64	51	6	2	5
Percentage	25.29	32.27	26.09	6.06	12.83
Male	56	45	5	2	4
Percentage	87.5	88.24	83.33	100	80
Female	16	14	1	0	1
Percentage	12.5	11.76	16.67	0	20
Unemployed	37	24	2	5	6
Percentage	14.63	15.2	8.79	15.25	15.37
Male	21	11	1	4	5
Percentage	56.76	45.83	50	80	83.33
Female	16	13	1	1	1
Percentage	43.24	54.17	50	20	16.67

Sources: Field Survey 2005-06.
0: Nil

5.5, Yunchuchu with 1: 5, and Bhandari with 1: 3, are above the sample ratio and the state's ratio.

(g) Health Institutions: There are 4 dispensaries, one in each sample villages giving first aid to the villagers. No doctors are available in any of these sample villages; however, there is 9 medical staff in the rank of compounder, nurse and others. Except for Longsa village, which have 4 such staff, all other villages have just one staff each. The average ratio of medical staff and the people is 1:809.44 for the sample villages. The table clearly shows that in Longsa one medical staff takes care of 1312.5 people (1:1312.5) that is lower than the sample village's ratio, district ratio and state's ratio. However, Yunchuchu with 1: 844 for, Sunglup with 1: 880 for and Bhandari 1: 311 are above the district and state's ratio. Thus, if we take the sample average ratio as the required ratio, then we find that there is a need for increasing the medical staff in the villages. This is because, except for Bhandari village, all other village is below the average ratio.

The Sample Households

The variation that exists among the villages in terms of demography, sanitation, housing, electricity, education etc from the sample households are explained below. A total of 99 household was surveyed from the four mentioned sample villages, 68 households from Longsa village, 9 households from Yunchuchu village, 12 households from Sunglup village and 10 households from Bhandari village.

1. Demographic characteristic of the Sample Population

From the total of 99 households surveyed, the total population of the universe is 393. From the Table 2.2 it can be seen that among the villages, Longsa village with 259 persons accounted for 65.9% of the total population followed by Bhandari, Yunchuchu and Sunglup with 54, 42 and 38 persons respectively. Their respective percentage share in the total population is 13.74% for Bhandari village, 10.69% for Yunchuchu and 9.67% for Sunglup village. From the table given below, discussions are done here in this section on household size, sex ratio, literacy and the sectoral employment in comparison with the sample villages, districts and the state.

(a) Household size: The average household size of the sample population as given in Table 2.2 is 3.97 persons that are lower than the average household size of the sample villages (7.44), district (6.23) and the state (6.1). Among the villages Bhandari village exhibits the highest family size with 5.4 persons, which is the reverse of the figure shown in the sample villages table with 3.24 persons and being the lowest. Yunchuchu village followed next with 4.67 persons that are more than half the size as provided by the VDB. Longsa and Sunglup villages are at the bottom with 3.97 persons and 3.81 persons respectively. In these villages the family size as provided by VDB are double the size of the actual findings.

(b) Sex ratio: From Table 2.2 it is seen that for the sample population male population accounts for 172 persons and female population accounts for 221 persons showing us a sex ratio of 1284 females per thousand males. The ratio is higher than the figure given by the sample village, the district and the state. However, findings from the sample population are close to the information given by the VDB as both the analysis shows a higher female population than male population. Among the villages Longsa village tops in terms of sex ratio with 1443 females per thousand males, followed by Yunchuchu with 1333 females per thousand males, Sunglup with 1111 females per thousand males and Bhandari with 800 female per thousand males. The findings from the sample population shows that except for Bhandari village all other village have a higher female population, which is the same as given by the VDB report.

(c) Literacy rate: Out of the total 316 people that are above the 7 years of age, 228 people are literate giving a percentage of 73.25 as the literacy rate for the sample population. The rate is above the state literacy rate (67.11%) but below the district literacy rate (81.28%). Among the villages Bhandari village has the highest

literacy rate with 86.11% higher than the rate of the sample population, the district and the state. Yunchuchu village with 79.41% have the rate that is lower the district but higher than the sample population and the state rate. The next is Longsa with 71.29% of literacy rate that is lower than the rate of the sample population and the district but higher than the state rate. The lowest literacy rate is shown by Sunglup with 56.76% that is lower then the rate of the sample population, district and the state.

Gender-wise literacy rate shows that male literacy rate is 83.92% of the sample male population, which is higher than the state's male literacy rate but lower than the district male literacy rate. For female literacy rate the percentage is 64.48% of the sample female population that is also higher than the state rate but lower than the district rate. Bhandari village exhibit a higher literacy rate for both male (92.59%) and female (84.21%) that is higher than the rate of the sample population, district and the state. For Yunchuchu village male literacy rate with 90.91% that is higher than the rate of the sample population, the district and the state. However, the female literacy rate with 73.91% exhibits a higher rate than the rate of the sample population and the state but lower than the district rate. For Longsa village male literacy rate is 82.95% that is higher than the state rate but lower than the rate of the sample population and the district rate. The female literacy rate is 68.81% that is higher than the rate of the sample population and the state but lower than the district rate. Sunglup village has 70% of male and 45% of female literacy rate, which is lower than the rate of the sample population, district and the state. Thus, the figure clearly exhibits that like that of the state and the district, the sample population also shows a higher male literacy rate over the female rate.

(d) Occupation: The workers constitute 64.38% of the total sample population, which is higher than the state and district percentage of workforce. Out of this total workforce agriculturalist constitute 60.08% that is lower than the state and the district percentage. More over, 25.29% of the total workforces are engaged in Non-agricultural activities, which is lower than the state and district percentage. The remaining 14.24% are unemployed.

Sunglup and Bhandari which has a total workforce of 86.84% and 72.5% respectively show a higher percentage of work forces than the sample, district and the state. However, Longsa with 61% and Yunchuchu with 54.76% of the total workforce exhibits a lower average than the sample average but higher than the state and the district workforce. The proportion of population engaged in agricultural activities are, Sunglup with 78.79% tops among the villages followed by Bhandari with 71.8%. These two villages exhibit a higher proportion of people engaged in agricultural activities over the average proportion of the sample population, the district and the state. While, Sunglup with 65.22% and Longsa with 52.53% shows a lower proportion of people engaged in agriculture than the district and the state average. However, a Sunglup village shows a higher average proportion than the sample population. In the case of non-agricultural activities, Longsa shows a higher proportion of population with 32.22% that is higher than the sample average proportion and state but lower than the district average proportion. The rest of the villages, viz., Yunchuchu with 26.09%, Bhandari with 12.83% and Sunglup with 6.06%, shows a lower average proportion of population engaged in non-agricultural activities that is lower than the state, district and the sample proportion. However, for Yunchuchu village, the proportion is higher than the sample proportion. In unemployment, Bhandari has the highest percentage with 15.37%, followed by Sunglup and Longsa villages with 15.25% and 15.2% respectively, all these three villages exhibits a higher rate than the sample proportion. For Yunchuchu, the percentage is low with 9% of its sample population being unemployed, which is lower than the average sample population.

The gender-wise occupation pattern shows that 74.34% of the total sample female populations are engaged in agricultural and allied activities, while only 25.66% of male populations are engaged in this sector. However, for non-agricultural sector male dominate with 87.5% of male population engaged in this sector as compared with that female with 12.5%. The unemployment rate among males is 56.76% that is higher than the female percentage of 43.24%. The village level gender-wise occupational pattern shows that female dominate the agricultural sector in all the villages, that is, Longsa with 84.34%, Yunchuchu with 80%, Sunglup with 61.54% and Bhandari with 53.57% of the total workforce are engaged in agricultural activities. However, for Sunglup and Bhandari villages, male's percentage in agricultural sector is also high with 38.46% and 46.43% respectively. In non-agricultural activities, male percentage is higher than female percentage in all the villages. The highest is in Sunglup village with 100% of the workforce engaged in non-agricultural activities being male followed by Longsa with 88.24%, Yunchuchu with 83.33% and Bhandari with 80% of the workforce being male. The female contribution in this sector is low in all the villages, viz., Longsa with 11.76%, Yunchuchu with 16.67%, Bhandari with 20% and Sunglup having no female engaged in this sector. The highest incidence of unemployment is among the males population in all villages. The village-wise male unemployment shows that Bhandari village has the highest unemployment with 83.33% followed by Sunglup with 80%, Yunchuchu with 50% and Longsa with 45.83%. Among the female unemployed, Longsa village exhibits highest with 54.17% followed by Yunchuchu with 50%, Sunglup with 20%and Bhandari with 16.67% each.

2. Physical and Social infrastructure of the sample household

The analysis of physical and social infrastructure of the sample households are given in the Table 2.3.

(a) Housing: From the table 2.3 it can be seen that 6 households has a pucca house accounting for 6.06% of the total houses, which is far below the district average of 18.90%. The highest percentage of pucca houses is in Sunglup with 16.67% of the total houses, followed by Longsa village with 5.88%. However, no pucca houses

Table 2.3
Physical and Social infrastructure

Category	*Total Sample household*		*Longsa*		*Yunchuchu*		*Sunglup*		*Bhandari*	
	No	%	No	%	No	%	No	%	No	%
Total households	99	100	68	100	9	100	12	100	10	100
Pucca House	6	6.06	4	5.88	0	0	2	16.67	0	0
Semi-pucca house	27	27.27	19	27.9	4	44.44	1	8.3	3	30
Kutcha house	66	66.67	45	66.2	5	65.66	9	75	7	70
Household with electricity facility	79	79.79	58	85.3	8	88.9	6	50	7	70
Household without electricity facility	20	20.21	10	14.7	1	11.1	6	50	3	30
River as a source of drinking water	99	100	68	100	9	100	12	100	10	100
Households that has Proper sanitation	29	29.29	17	25	3	33.3	5	41.7	4	40
Households that does not have proper sanitation	70	70.71	51	75	6	66.7	7	58.3	6	60

Source: Field Survey 2005-06.
0: Nil

are found in Yunchuchu and Bhandari villages. Further, the semi-pucca houses account for 27.27% that is also lower than the district average of 59.06%. Village-wise comparison reveals that Yunchuchu with 44.44% exhibit the highest percentage of semi-house that is higher than the average sample household but lower than the district average. Bhandari with 30% and Longsa with 27.94% also show a higher percentage than the average sample households but lower than the district average. However, Sunglup with 8.33% exhibits a low percentage that is lower than both the average sample household and district average. Thus majority of the villagers have a Kutcha houses that accounts for 66.67% of the total houses. Sunglup has the highest percentage of kutcha houses with 75%, followed by Bhandari with 70%, Longsa with 66.18% and Yunchuchu with 55.56%.

(b) Sanitation: From the total of 99 households surveyed only 29 households have proper sanitation accounting for 29.29% of the total availability of sanitation as shown in Table 2.3. The result is far below the district average of 63.38% and the state's average of 57%. Sunglup with 41.67% tops in terms of sanitation followed by Bhandari with 40% and Yunchuchu with 33.33%. At the bottom lies Longsa village with 25% of the households having sanitation facility.

(c) Water: The source of drinking water for all the sample households is well, stream and rainwater harvest.

(d) Electricity: In terms of the availability of electricity facility Table 2.3 reveals that 79 households in the sample villages have been electrified that accounted for 79.79% of the total households. Village-wise data reveals that Yunchuchu is having the highest percentage of electrified households (88.89%) followed by Longsa with 85.29% and Bhandari with 70%. On the other extreme, Sunglup is having the lowest percentage with 50%.

The socio-economic profile of the study areas reveals that a lot more needs to be done to improve people's standard of living. In the field of physical infrastructure, all weathered road, electricity connectivity, transport and communication and the access to banking system need to be emphasized because this infrastructure facilitates the production sector like agriculture, industry, trade, etc. Moreover, equal importance needs to be given to improve the social infrastructure because it enhance human welfare, freedom from ignorance, diseases and fear etc. The improvement in these sectors will directly or indirectly reduce the poverty level in the state.

NOTES

1. Todaro, M.P. (1998), *"Economic Development"*, 6th edition, Addison-Wesley Reading, Massachusetts, p.394.
2. Government of Nagaland, Breif history of the district, p1. Online [Available] www.wokha.nic.in 2007.
3. Sharma, K.C. (1994), *Poverty, Unemployment and Inequalities in Tribal India; With Special Reference to Himachal Pradesh*, Reliance Publishing House, New Delhi, p.97.
4. Government of India (2001), *Provisional Population Total; rural-urban distribution*, Census of India, Directorate of Census Operations, Nagaland, p.5.
5. Government of Nagaland (2004), *State Human Development Report 2004*, Department of Planning and Coordination, Nagaland, p.15.
6. *Ibid.* 16.
7. Jamir, K (2006), "Status of Infrastructure in Nagaland: Strategies to Strengthen Infrastructures for Economic Development", In NUTA (ed.) 2006, *Economic Development in Nagaland, Constraints and Prospects*, p. 234.
8. *Ibid.* 18.

3

Assessment of Nutrition and MPCE

In this chapter the nutritional requirement by different age and income groups among the rural population of Wokha district has been analysed. The monthly per capita expenditure (MPCE) on food and non-food has been estimated and discussed here in this section. Further more, the calorie intake and its relationship with family size and monthly per capita expenditure (MPCE) has been explained.

Calorie Intake

The national aggregate daily calorie requirement is calculated by summing up the nutritional intake across all individuals. The average calorie intake is then calculated by dividing the national aggregate of daily calorie intake with the total population. The measurement of food security at the national level entails the calculation of the extent to which the production of the staple food in a country can provide the nutritional minimum of 2047 Kcal per day for the rural population and 2020 Kcal per day for the urban population in 2004-05.[43] To arrive at the calorie norms for the sample population, the data on household consumption of various food items were collected from four villages of Wokha district in 2005-06. The food items that were covered by the survey are as follows rice, fruits (fresh and dry), vegetables, meat, fish, egg, milk, sugar, salt, oils, etc. The reference periods used for collection of these data is for 30 days prior to the survey. The collected data on consumption of food items were converted into calorie using the conversion table provided by the NSSO report 513. Again basing on the NSSO division of age group, the per capita calorie intake of different ages and sex groups were calculated. From the table no. 3.1 and figure 1, it is clear that the average calorie intake of the rural sample population for the year 2005 – 06 is 2441.92 Kcal per person per day, which is higher than both the average calorie intake of 2044 Kcal for the rural areas in Nagaland and the National average for rural area of 2047 Kcal per person per day for the year 2004-05 by 16.3% and 16.17% respectively.

Table 3.1
Estimated Calorie Norms

Category	*Average Rural calorie norms (Kcal per person per day)*
*National calorie norms (2004-05)	2047
*Nagaland Norms (2004-05)	2044
Sample survey Norms (2005-06)	2441.92

Sources: *NSSO Report 508 and Field Survey 2005-06.

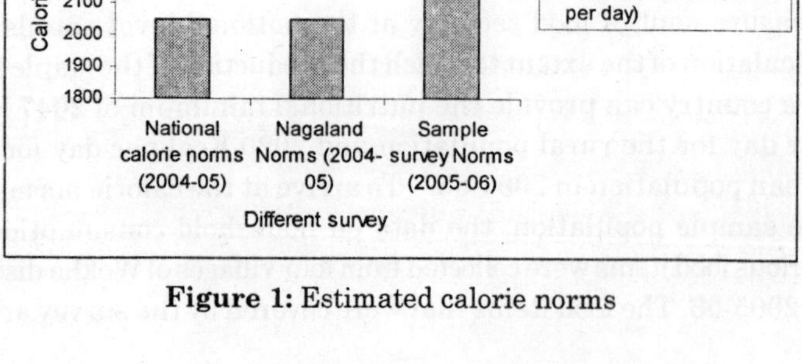

Figure 1: Estimated calorie norms

1. Average Calorie Intake per day by age and sex groups

Nutritional requirement vary from person to person depending on age and gender. Thus, calorie intake by different age and sex group per person per day are shown in the table given below.

Table 3.2
Average calorie intake by Age and Sex Groups

Age group (in years)	*Average calorie intake (Kilo calorie per day)*		*Sex groups average calorie intake in Kcal per day*		*Per-centage difference by gender*
	Average	*% to total*	*Male*	*Female*	
Over all	2441.92	100	2427.48	2453.16	1.06
<1	246.6	0.92	406.79	175.41	131.91
1 – 3	973.66	3.65	936.92	1036.11	10.59
4 – 6	1816.99	6.81	1742.06	1869.88	7.34
7 – 9	2036.19	7.63	2301.63	1848.82	24.49
10 – 12	2408.42	9.02	2915.67	2252.34	29.45
13 – 15	2842.36	10.65	2797.54	2877.03	2.84
16 – 19	2862.29	10.73	3042.57	2700.04	12.69
20 – 39	2916.92	10.93	2847.99	2968.87	4.24
40 – 49	2918.79	10.94	2812.23	3036.14	7.96
50 – 59	2829.45	10.6	2860.37	2807.63	1.88
60 – 69	2597.16	9.73	2513.59	2634.77	4.82
70 and above	2239.14	8.39	2323.18	2127.1	9.22

Sources: Field Survey 2005-06.

It may be observed from the Table 3.2 that the average calorie intake per person per day for the sample population as a whole is 2441.92 Kcal. The significant difference in calorie intake amongst different age group is evident from the table and figure 2. As such, the lower age group shows a much lower per capita calorie intake than the older age group for both the sexes due to the obvious reason. As we move on to higher age groups, the average calorie intake increases up to age group of 40-49 years and thereafter it declines. The figures in the table indicate that, for the age group of 1 year and below, the calorie intake is estimated at an average of 246.6 Kcal, for the group 1-3 years it is 973.66 Kcal, for the group 4-6 years it is 1816.99 Kcal, for the group 7-9 years it is 2036.19 Kcal, for the group 10-12 years it is 2408.42 Kcal, for the group 13-15 it is 2842.36 kcal, for the group 16-19 years it is 2862.29 Kcal, for the group 20-39 years it is 2916.92 Kcal and it rose to 2918.79 Kcal for the age group of 40-49 years. From there on, it declines to 2829.45 Kcal for the age group of 50-59 years, 2597.16 kcal for the age group of 60-69 years and 2239.14 Kcal for 70 years and above. The analysis reveals that there is a consistent increase in percentage share of per capita calorie intake across the age group of 1 year and below (.92%) to 40-49 years (10,94%). From thereon, it declines to 10.6%, 9.73% and 8,39% for the age group of 50-60 years, 60-69 years and 70 years and above respectively.

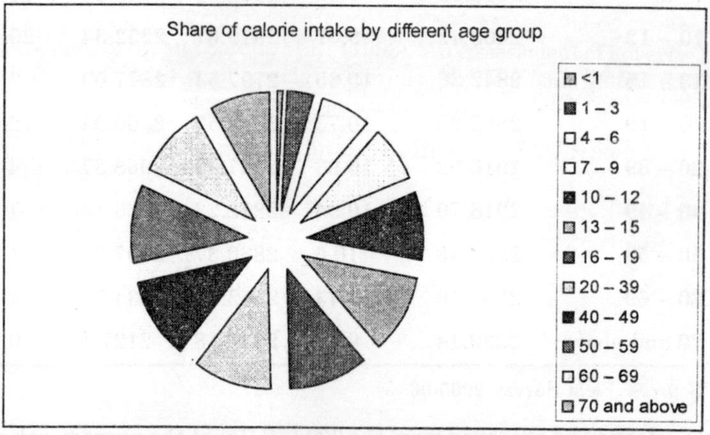

Figure 2: Percentage share of different age groups.

The sex-wise data are less consistent than the population average, yet both the consumption data display similar trends as shown in figure 3. The sex-wise sample population calorie intake shows that the average calorie intake per person per day among the female population is 2453.16 Kcal that is marginally higher than the average calorie intake of male population (2427.48 Kcal) by1.06%. It further suggests that for the age group 1 year and below, male average calorie intake per day is significantly higher than female average calorie intake by131.91%. For the age group 7-9 years, 10-12 years, 16-19 years, 50-59 years and 70 years and above, the average calorie intake of male is higher than the female by 24.49%, 29.45%, 12.69%, 1.88% and 9.22% respectively. Whereas, for the age group 1-3 years, 4-6 years, 13-15 years, 20-39 years, 40-49 years and 60-69 years, the average calorie intake of female is higher than male by 10.59%, 7.34%, 2.84%, 4.24%, 7.96% and 9.22% respectively.

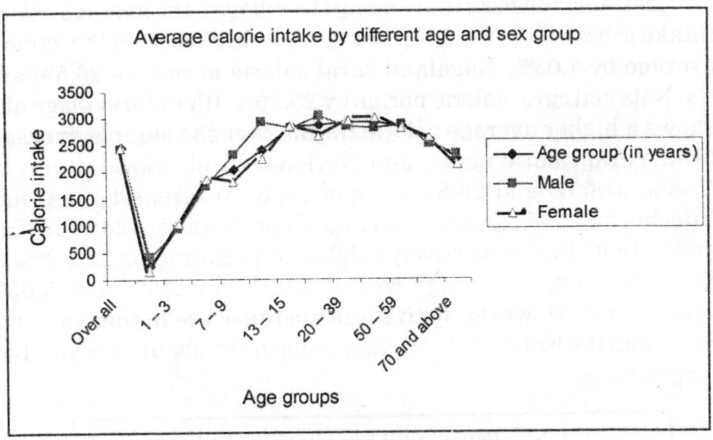

Figure 3: Calorie intake by age and sex groups.

2. *Village-wise Average calorie intake*

Apart from the individual calorie intake per person per day, village-wise average calorie intakes are also depicted here. The figure in Table 3.3 and figure no. 4 shows the calorie intake per person per day for the sample villages of Wokha district, Nagaland.

Table 3.3
Average calorie intake of the sample villages

Category	*Average Calorie intake (in Kcal)*	*Percentage (%) difference to total average*	*Male calorie intake*	*Female calorie intake*	*Percentage (%) difference by Gender*
All villages	2441.92	100	2427.48	2453.16	1.06
Longsa	2428.59	-0.55	2443.98	2417.94	1.07
Yunchuchu	2318.97	-5.03	2086.29	2493.46	19.52
Sunglup	2613.65	+7.03	2544.62	2675.78	5.15
Bhandari	2480.59	+1.58	2503.61	2451.82	2.11

Sources: Field Survey 2005-06.

The table suggests that among the villages, the average calorie intake is highest in Sunglup village. It is higher than the sample average by 7.03%, Nagaland rural calorie norms by 26.5% and the National rural calorie norms by 26.29%. Bhandari village also shows a higher average calorie intake over the sample average, State rural calorie norms and National rural calorie norms by 1.58%, 21.05% and 20.87% respectively. Whereas Longsa and Yunchuchu villages with an average calorie intake of 2428.59 Kcal and 2318.97 Kcal respectively exhibit lower average calorie intake than the sample average calorie intake by .55% and 5.03% respectively. However, both these averages are higher than the State and the National rural calorie norms by about 18% and 14% respectively.

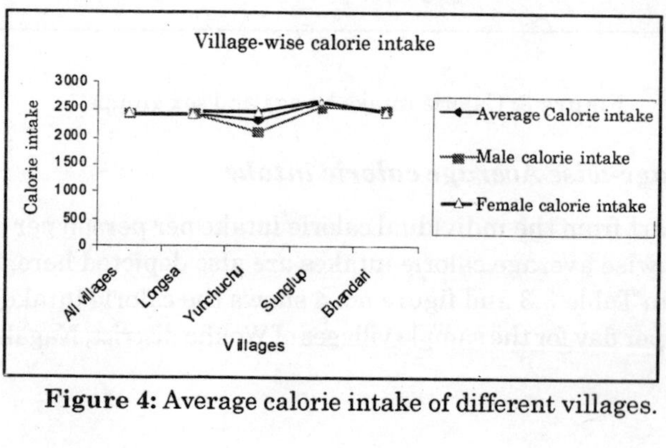

Figure 4: Average calorie intake of different villages.

Gender-wise average calorie intake analysis shows that on an average, female average calorie intake are higher than male by a margin of 1.06%. Village-wise average calorie intake by gender as depicted in the above table and figure shows that the average calorie intake of male is higher than that of female in Longsa and Bhandari villages by 1.07% and 2.11% respectively. Whereas, in Sunglup and Yunchuchu villages, the average calorie intake of female is higher than male by 5.15% and 19.52% respectively.

3. Range-wise Average calorie intake

The figured in Table 3.4 and figure no. 5 shows the calorie intake per person per day for the sample ranges of Wokha district, Nagaland.

Table 3.4
Average calorie intake of different ranges

Category	*Average Calorie intake*	*Percentage difference to total average*	*Male calorie intake*	*Female calorie intake*	*Percentage difference by Gender*
All ranges	2441.92	100	2427.48	2453.16	1.06
Upper range	2428.59	-0.55	2443.98	2417.94	1.07
Middle range	2458.94	0.69	2315.46	2576.33	11.27
Lower range	2480.59	1.58	2503.61	2451.82	2.11

Sources: Field survey 2005-06.

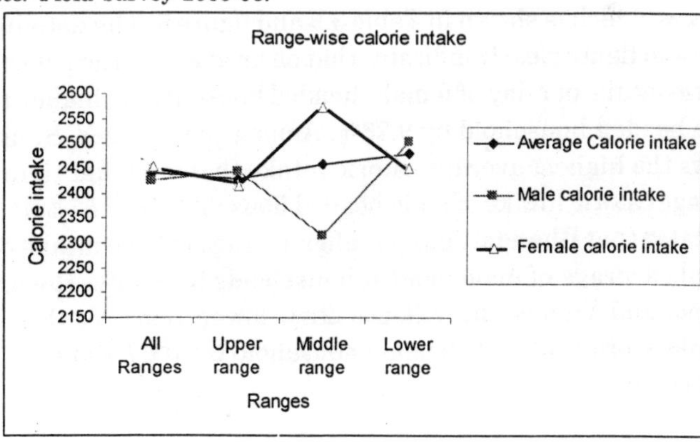

Figure 5: Average calorie intake of different ranges.

The table suggests that among the ranges, the average calorie intake is highest in Lower range. It is higher than the sample average by 1.58%, State rural calorie norms and National rural calorie norms by 21.05% and 20.87% respectively. Middle range with an average calorie intake of 2458.94 Kcal per person per day also shows a higher average calorie intake than the sample average by .69%, State rural calorie norms and National rural calorie norms by 16.75% and 16.87% respectively. However, Upper range with an average calorie intake of 2428.59 Kcal exhibit lower average calorie intake than the sample average calorie intake by .55%. But the average calorie intake is higher than the State and the National rural calorie norms by about 18%.

Gender-wise average calorie intake analysis shows that on an average, female average calorie intake are higher than male by a margin of 1.06%. Range-wise average calorie intake by gender as depicted in the above table and figure shows that the average calorie intake of male is higher than that of female in upper and lower by 1.07% and 2.11% respectively. However, in Middle range, the average calorie intake of female is higher than male by 11.27%.

4. Average calorie intake by Sex-wise head of the Household

An analysis is done to show the variation in the average calorie intake by female and male headed households of the sample villages, which is shown in Table 3.5 and figure 6. The data in the table and figure clearly indicates that on an average, the per capita calorie intake per day of female-headed household is higher than male headed household by 9.78%. Among the villages, Sunglup shows the highest average calorie intake that is higher than the average calorie intake of male headed household by 6.57%. It also indicates that Bhandari has a higher average calorie intake than sample average of male headed households by 1.46%. However, Longsa and Yunchuchu villages show lowrr averages than the sample average of male headed household by -0.67% and. 4.31% respectively.

Table 3.5
Male and female headed household average calorie intake per day

Category	*Average Calorie Intake per day (Kcal)*					
	Total Average	*Male headed house-hold*	*Percentage difference to total male*	*Female headed house-hold*	*Per-centage difference to total female*	*Per-centage difference by sex of head*
All villages	2441.92	2374.04	100	2606.26	100	9.78
Longsa	2428.59	2358.25	-0.67	2715.59	+4.19	15.15
Yunchuchu	2318.97	2271.71	-4.31	2437.11	-6.49	7.92
Sunglup	2613.65	2530.13	+6.57	2983.51	+14.47	17.92
Bhandari	2480.59	2408.62	+1.46	1987.6	-23.74	21.18

Sources: Field Survey 2005-06.

For the female headed household, the Table 3.5 shows that the average calorie intake per day in Longsa and Sunglup villages are higher than the average calorie intake of female headed households by 4.19% and 14.47% respectively. While Yunchuchu and Bhandari villages have average calorie intake that are lower than the average of female headed household by 6.49% and 23.74% respectively.

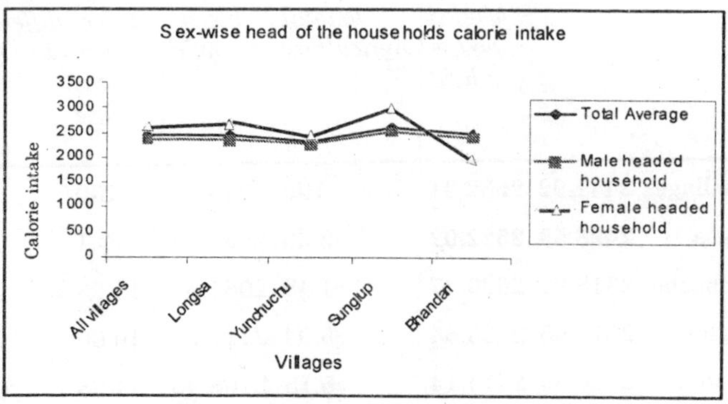

Figure 6: Average calorie intake by sex-wise head of household.

In comparison, the result shows that on an average, the calorie intakes of female headed households are higher than the male headed households by 9.78%. Among the villages, the female headed households in Longsa, Sunglup and Yunchuchu have higher average calorie intake per day than male headed household by 15.15%, 17.92% and 7.28% respectively. It is only in Bhandari village the average calorie intake is higher in male headed households than female headed households by 21.18%. The result suggests that female headed household is nutritionally better off.

5. Average calorie intake by occupation-wise head of the Household

The households have been segregated based on the occupation of the head of the family as Agricultural and Service headed households. Thereafter, estimate their average calorie intake and the extent of variation amongst the selected categories which are shown in the given table and figure below.

Table 3.6
Agriculture and Service headed household Average calorie intake per day

Category	*Average Calorie Intake per day (Kcal)*					
	Total Average	*Agri- culture headed house- hold*	*Percentage difference to total Agriculture*	*Service headed house- hold*	*Per- centage differ- ence to total Service*	*Per- centage difference by Occu- pation of head*
All villages	2441.92	2582.31	100	2455.2	100	5.18
Longsa	2428.59	2522.02	-2.33	2531.43	+3.1	0.37
Yunchuchu	2318.97	2620.47	+1.48	2081.34	-15.23	25.9
Sunglup	2613.65	2735.54	+5.94	2717.68	+10.66	0.66
Bhandari	2480.59	2715.14	+5.15	2168.45	-11.68	25.21

Sources: Field Survey 2005-06.

From the table above it can be seen that the average calorie intake of agricultural headed households is higher than the service headed households by 1.05%. The village-wise data shows that among the agricultural headed households, Sunglup have a higher average calorie intake than the average calorie intake of the agricultural headed households by 5.94%. It is followed by Bhandari and Yunchuchu with 2715.14 Kcal and 2620.47 Kcal of calorie intake, that are above the average of the agricultural headed households by 5.15% and 1.48% respectively. While Longsa exhibits the lowest average calorie intake among the villages that is lower than the average by 2.33%.

In respect of the service headed households, figure 7 and table 3.6 shows that Sunglup has the highest average calorie intake that is followed by Longsa whose averages are higher average than the average of the service headed households. However, Yunchuchu and Bhandari exhibit lower average than the average calorie intake of the service headed households by 15.23% and 11.68% respectively.

The inter-village variation in average calorie intake between the agricultural and service headed households shows that in Yunchuchu, Sunglup and Bhandari, the agricultural headed households are higher than the service headed households by 25.9%, 0.66% and 25.21% respectively. However, in Longsa the average calorie intake of service is higher than agricultural headed households by 0.37%.

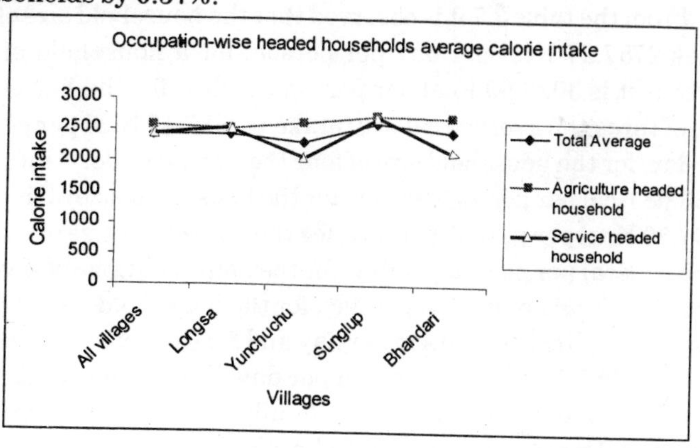

Figure 7: Average calorie intake by occupation-wise head of household.

6. Family size and Calorie intake

The relationship between calorie intake and the household size are explained by the Table 3.7 and figure 8 given below.

Table 3.7

Family size and average daily Calorie intake

Average Family size (X)	*Average No. of children **	*average no. of adult***	*Average calorie intake (Y)*
1 person	0	1	2757.27
2 persons	0	2	3023.7
3 persons	0.812	2.187	2687.18
4 persons	0.823	3.118	2433.09
5 persons	2.37	2.63	2297.81
6 persons	2.71	3.29	2185.92
7 persons	4.33	2.67	2645.64
8 persons	3	5	2579.54
10 persons	7	3	1987.54

Sources: Field Survey 2005-06.
* Persons under 15 years of age.
** Persons 15 years and above.

From the table 3.7 it is observed that the household size of one takes 2757.27 Kcal per day per person, for a household of two persons it is 3023.69 Kcal per person per day, for the household size of three the average calorie intake is 2687.17 Kcal per person per day, for the household size of four the average calorie intake is 2433.08 Kcal per person per day, for the household size of five it is 2297.80 Kcal per person per day, for the household size of six it is 2185.91 Kcal per person per day, for the household size of seven it is 2645.63 Kcal per person per day, for the household size of eight it is 2579.53 Kcal per person per day and for the household size of ten it is 1987.56 Kcal per person per day. The table reveals that on an average, as the size of the family goes on increasing the average calorie intake goes on declining.

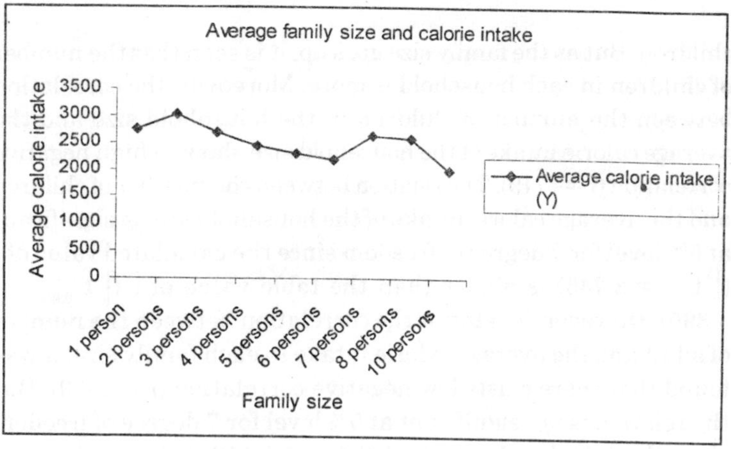

Figure 8: Family size and average calorie intake.

To examine whether the hypothesis 'higher family size, lower is the calorie intake' holds true or otherwise, the correlation between the two variables (household size and calorie intake) is evaluated using Karl Pearson methods of Correlation. The solution for correlation gives,

$r = -0.703$

The result shows that the correlation coefficient value is negative. This indicates that there exists an inverse relation between the calorie intake and family size. To find whether the correlation coefficient is significant at 5% level, t-test for the given distribution is undertaken. The calculated value of t comes out to be $|t| = 2.63$ whereas the table value $|t_{0.05}| = 1.895$. Since the calculated value is higher than the table value, the correlation is significant at 5% level for 7 degrees of freedom. Therefore, the hypothesis is accepted. Hence higher the family size, lower will be the calorie intake.

The reason why in higher family size, the average calorie intake is lower can be explained by looking at the number of children in each family size. The figure in Table 3.7 shows that lower family size, especially family size of 1 and 2, have zero children. But as the family size goes up, it is seen that the number of children in each household is more. Moreover, the correlation between the number of children in the household size and the average calorie intake of the household size shows a high negative correlation (r = -.719). The relation between the number of children and the average calorie intake of the household size is significant at 5% level for 7 degree of freedom since the calculated value of t ($|t|$ = 2.745) is higher than the table value of t ($|t_{0.05}|$ = 1.895). However, looking at the correlation between the number of adult and the average calorie intake in each family size, it was found that there exists low negative correlation (r = -.389). But the relation is not significant at 5% level for 7 degree of freedom since the calculated value of t ($|t|$ = 1.119) is lower than the table value of t ($|t_{0.05}|$ = 1.895). Thus we accept that the lower average calorie intake in higher family size is due to the presence of higher number of children as the family size goes up. The obvious reason is that the average calorie requirements for children are always lower than that of an adult in any given normal circumstances.

To measure the effect on calorie intake from a change in family size has been analysed through simple regression method. Regression equation of Y on X is; Y-Mean of Y = byx (X- Mean of X)

$$Y = 2901.497 - 76.43X$$

Where, y is the calorie intake and x is the family size. This result shows that the regression coefficient 'byx' of Y on X is -76.43. The negative value of the regression coefficient indicates that the relation between y and x is indirect. This shows that a unit change in the family size (X) will have an impact on the calorie intake of the people (Y) by -76.43 times. To see whether the regression analysis is significant or not, t-test is undertaken. The result shows that the calculated value of t ($|t|$ = 2.64) is much higher than the table value ($|t_{0.05}|$ = 1.895), therefore, the value of b is significant at 5% level for 7 degrees of freedom. Hence a small change in family size will have a large negative impact on calorie intake of the people.

7. Calorie intake and income

It is common experience that a person with higher income tends to have better diet and vice versa. Thus, it is vital to examine the relation between these two variables. Table 3.8 and figure 9 shows the per capita monthly income and average daily calorie intake for different income groups.

Table 3.8
Average calorie intake and monthly income

Group No	*Income Group (Rs.)*	*No. of HH*	*Total No. of person*	*Per capita daily calorie intake*	*Per capita monthly income (Rs.)*
1	1 - 500	55	186	2408.58	258.89
2	501 - 1000	24	121	2481.54	761.72
3	1001 - 2000	16	70	2430.02	1271.29
4	2001 - 3000	2	11	2665.4	2581.82
5	3001 - 4000	1	1	2927.4	3100
6	4001 and above	1	4	2266.6	5194.25

Sources: Field Survey 2005-06.

From the Table 3.8, it can be seen that as the average income goes on increasing, the average calorie intake shows a fluctuating trend. The calorie intake per person per day for the lowest income group of Rs.1 to Rs. 500 per capita per month is 2408.58 Kcal. The next group follows with the calorie intake of 2481.54 Kcal per person per day but decreased to 2430.02 Kcal per person per day for the next income group. However, in the fourth income group the calorie intake rose to 2665.4 Kcal per person per day and increased to 2927.4 Kcal per person per day in the 5th group. For the highest income group the calorie intake is the lowest with 2266.6 Kcal per person per day. It appears that there is a fluctuating relationship between the two variables.

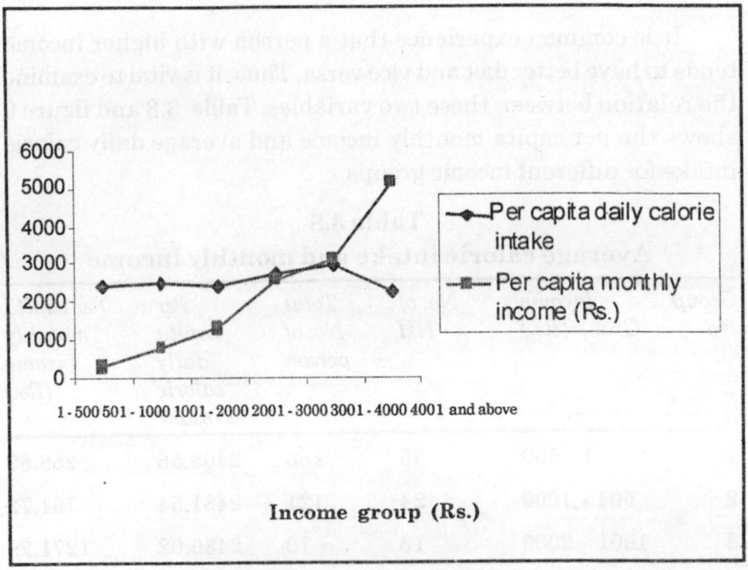

Figure 9: Average calorie intake and monthly income

The relationship between per capita income and per capita calorie intake can best be ascertained by finding the correlation between the two. The correlation solution shows,

r = .0089

The value of correlation coefficient is closer to 0, therefore there is no linear relationship between the variables. To find whether the correlation coefficient is significant, t-test for the given distribution is done. Since he calculated value of t (t = .0178) is less than $t_{0.05,}$ we conclude that there is no significant relationship between the two given variables. Thus, the hypothesis which states that higher the income of the people, higher is the calorie intake does not hold true in this case. The result clearly violates the common experience that people take higher calories as their income increases under normal circumstances. However, the information about the monthly income as provided by the interviewee cannot be considered as reliable because of two reasons. Firstly, people in the rural areas does not keep any record of their monthly income, thus reliable data at the household level is not available. Secondly, people seldom tell their true monthly income to any interviewer. Hence, we cannot use this income while measuring poverty and instead Monthly Per Capita Expenditure (MPCE) is used.

Monthly Per Capita Expenditure (MPCE)

The Report of the Expert Group (1993) maintains that the household consumer expenditure is more reliable than income and hence more suitable for measuring poverty. The reliability of the consumption expenditure is well recognized.[44] Thus, Monthly Per Capita Expenditure is used as a proxy for the actual income while determining poverty.

To generate the total household expenditures, the aggregate of the sub-total of various consumption items were divided into two groups, viz, food items and non-food items. The expenditure on food items includes cereals and cereal substitutes, pulses and their products, edible oils, egg, fish meat, vegetables, sugar, salt and spices, beverages, processed food etc. While the data of households expenditure on foods, pan, tobacco and intoxicants, fuel and light, miscellaneous goods and services, including non-institutional medical care, rents and, taxes, cereals, egg, fish and meat, fruits (fresh and dry), conveyance etc. are collected over the last 30 days prior to the survey.[45] Valuation of consumption out of purchase is evaluated at the purchase price. Consumption out of home produce is evaluated at ex farm or ex factory rate. The average expenditure on this food items yield a poverty norm that could be called starvation line or food energy requirement. However, the starvation poverty norm is generally supplemented by some allowance on non-food consumption. Thus, the expenditure on non-food items are also calculated to arrived at the poverty line. The expenditure on non-food items include fuels and light, clothing and footwear, education, medical, miscellaneous consumer goods, pan, tobacco, intoxicants, rent etc. The household expenditures data on clothing, footwear, education, medical care and durable goods which are not frequent, are collected over the last 365 days prior to the survey, thereafter, the total is divided by 12 months so as to arrive at monthly average expenditure. Value of consumption out of gifts, loans, free collections, and goods received in exchange of goods and services is imputed at the rate of average local retail prices prevailing during the reference period. The MPCE or poverty line is arrived at by dividing the household expenditure on both food and non-food items by the number of person in each household[46].

1. Assessment of the Monthly Per Capita Expenditure (MPCE)

The data in the Table 3.9(a) and figure 10 show that the estimated monthly per capita expenditure for the sample population is Rs. 942.66 or Rs. 31.42 per person per day at 2005-06 prices, which is higher than National average of Rs. 558.78 per person per month or Rs. 18.63 per person per day at 2004-05 prices by 69% but lower than Nagaland state average of Rs. 1010.81 per person per month or Rs. 33.69 per person per day at 2004-05 prices by 7%. Out of this average (Rs. 942.60), 57% of the expenditure is made on markets while 43% of the expenditures come from their own product which goes unaccounted for an income.

Table 3.9 (a)
MPCE estimates

Category	*Average Rural MPCE (Rs.)*	*Average Rural Per Capita Per Day (Rs.)*
*National MPCE (at 2004-05 prices)	558.78	18.63
*Nagaland MPCE (at 2004-05 prices)	1010.81	33.69
**Sample survey MPCE (at 2005-06 prices)	942.60	31.42

Sources: *NSSO Report 508 and ** Field Survey 2005-06.

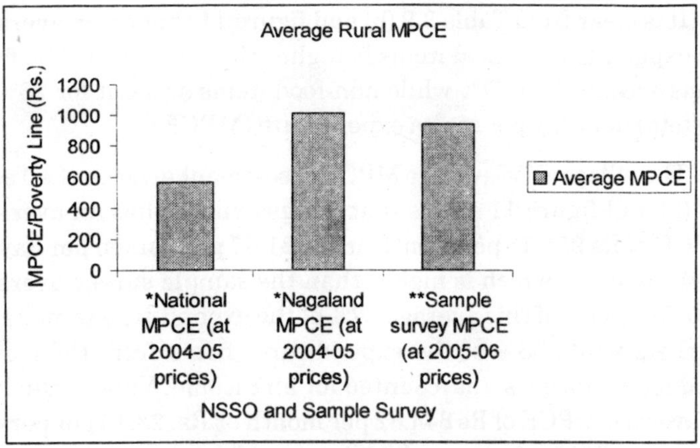

Figure 10: Estimated MPCE.

Table 3.9(b) and figure 11 shows the village-wise MPCE and the percentage share of food and non-food items in the total per capita monthly expenditure (MPCE).

Table 3.9 (b)
Share in average MPCE (village-wise)

Category	*Average MPCE (Rs.) (FE + NFE)*	*Average Per Capita Per Day (Rs.)*	*Share in MPCE by different items*				
			Share of FE		*Share of NFE*		*Village-wise Percentage (%) difference with the total MPCE average*
			Average (Rs.)	*(%)*	*Average (Rs.)*	*(%)*	
Villages	942.60	31.42	722.32	77	219.91	23	1
Longsa	950.18	31.67	709.71	75	240.47	25	+0.79
Yunchuchu	844.85	28.16	682.46	81	162.39	19	-10.38
Sunglup	866.82	28.89	752.34	87	114.48	13	-8.05
Bhandari	920.48	30.68	792.7	86	127.78	14	-2.35

Sources: Field Survey 2005-06.
FE: Food Expenditure.
NFE: Non-food Expenditure.

It is clear from Table 3.9 (b) and figure 11 that on an average the expenditure on food items is higher than non-food. The food items accounts for 77% while non-food items account for 23% of the total monthly per capita expenditure (MPCE).

The village-wise average MPCE assessment given in the Table 3.9 (b) and figure 11 shows that Longsa village has an average MPCE of Rs 950.18 per month or Rs. 31.67 per person per day at 2005-06 prices which is higher than the sample survey average by 0.79%. Out of this average 62% of the expenditure is made on markets while 38% of the expenditures come from their own product which goes unaccounted for an income. Yunchuchu has an average MPCE of Rs 844.82 per month or Rs. 28.16 per person per day at 2005-06 prices which is lower than the sample survey average by 10.38%. Out of this average 51% of the expenditure is made on markets while 49% of the expenditures come from their own product which goes unaccounted for an income. Sunglup has an average MPCE of Rs 866.82 per month or Rs. 28.89 per person per day at 2005-06 prices which is lower than the sample survey average by 8.05%. Out of this average 38% of the expenditure is made on markets while 62% of the expenditures come from their own product which goes unaccounted for an income. Bhandari has an average MPCE of Rs 920.48 per month or Rs. 30.68 per person per day at 2005-06 prices which is lower than the sample average by 2.35%. Out of this average 49% of the expenditure is made on markets while 51% of the expenditures come from their own product which goes unaccounted for an income.

The share of monthly per capita expenditure on food and non-food items for Longsa village is 75% and 25% respectively. It can be seen that the share of expenditure on non-food is highest among the villages and higher than the sample average as well. The share of per capita monthly expenditure on food and non-food items for the Yunchuchu village is 81% and 19% respectively. For Sunglup, the share of per capita monthly expenditure by food items with 87% exhibits the highest percentage share among the selected villages. While the share of per capita monthly expenditure on non-food items with 13% shows the lowest percentage share among the selected category. The share of per capita monthly expenditure on food and non-food items for Bhandari village is 86% and 14% respectively.

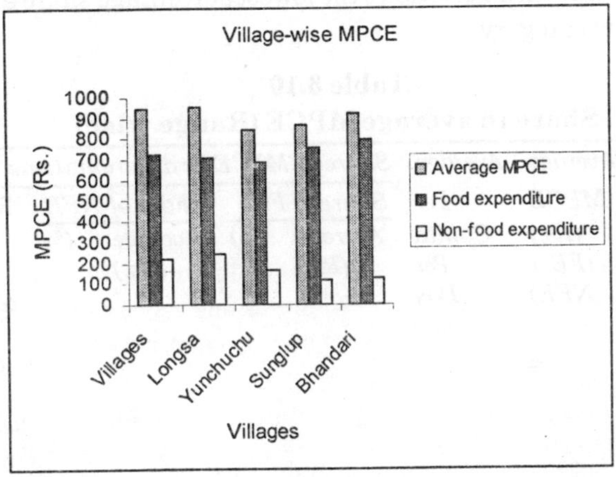

Figure 11: Village-wise MPCE and share of food and non-food expenditure

2. Range-wise decomposition of MPCE

The Range-wise average MPCE assessments given in the Table 3.10 and figure 12 show that Upper range has an average MPCE of Rs 950.18 per month or Rs. 31.67 per person per day at 2005-06 prices that is higher than the sample survey average by 0.79%, while Middle range has an average MPCE of Rs 907.54 per month or Rs. 30.25 per person per day at 2005-06 prices and Lower range has an average MPCE of Rs 920.48 per month or Rs. 30.68 per person per day at 2005-06 prices that are lower than the sample average by 3.72% and 2.35% respectively.

The share of monthly per capita expenditure on food and non-food items for the Upper range is 75% and 25% respectively. It can be seen that the share of expenditure on non-food is highest among the ranges and higher than the sample average as well. The share of per capita monthly expenditure on food and non-food items for the middle range is 79% and 23% respectively. For lower range, the share of per capita monthly expenditure by food items with 86% exhibits the highest percentage share among the selected ranges. While the share of per capita monthly expenditure on non-food items with 14% shows the lowest percentage share among the selected category.

Table 3.10
Share in average MPCE (Range wise)

Category	*Average MPCE (Rs.) (FE + NFE)*	*Average Per Capita Per Day (Rs.)*	*Share in MPCE by different items*				*Range-wise Percentage (%) difference with the total average*
			Share of FE		*Share of NFE*		
			Average (Rs.)	*(%)*	*Average (Rs.)*	*(%)*	
All Ranges	942.6	31.42	722.32	77	219.91	23	1
Upper	950.18	31.67	709.71	75	240.47	25	0.79
Middle	907.54	30.25	715.66	79	191.54	23	-3.72
Lower	920.48	30.68	792.7	86	127.78	14	-2.35

Sources: Field Survey 2005-06.
FE: Food Expenditure.
NFE: Non-food Expenditure

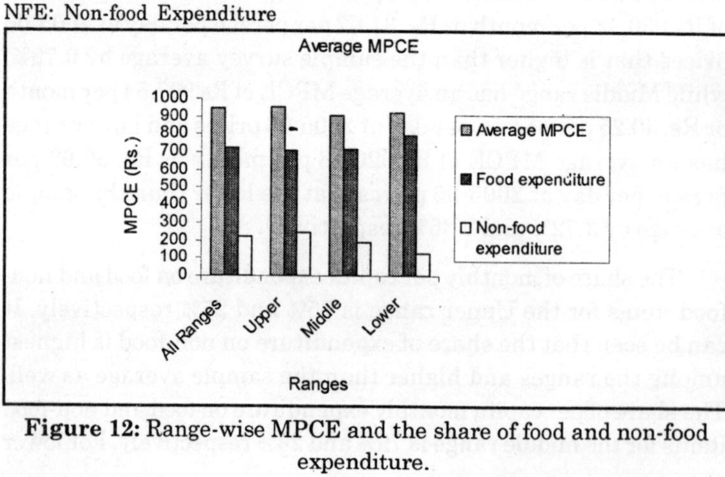

Figure 12: Range-wise MPCE and the share of food and non-food expenditure.

3. Decomposition of MPCE by Sex-wise Head of the Household

The differences in monthly MPCE among the male and female headed households and their allocation pattern and food and non-food items are explained in this section. The data in table no 3.11 and figure 13 (a) and (b) shows that the average MPCE of male headed household is Rs. 945.74 or Rs. 31.52 per person per day at 2005-06 prices, while it is Rs. 924.82 or Rs. 30.83 per person per day at 2005-06 prices with female headed households. This follows that the average MPCE for male headed household is higher than both the female headed household and the average of the sample survey by 2.26% and 0.33% respectively. This may be due to higher income earning opportunities for male, which leads to higher income resulting in higher MPCE for male headed households. For male headed households, the proportions of monthly expenditure on food and non-food items are 76% and 24% respectively. The corresponding shares of expenditure in the female headed households are 79% and 21% respectively. This indicates that despite having lower MPCE, in female headed households a greater proportion of their expenditure is made on food items as compared to male headed households. It may be due to the reason that when women have sole control over family resources, the expenditure on food items tend to be higher because they are more concern in providing better food to the family.

The village-wise MPCE for male headed households are given as follows; For Longsa it is Rs. 947.77 per month or Rs. 31.59 per person per day at 2005-06 prices, Yunchuchu has Rs. 879.81 per month or Rs. 29.33 per person per day at 2005-06 prices, Sunglup has Rs. 901.1 per month or Rs. 30.04 per person per day at 2005-06 prices and Bhandari has Rs. 1023.02 per month or Rs. 34.1 per person per day at 2005-06 prices. Among the total male headed households, Longsa and Bhandari villages exhibit higher MPCE than the average of total male headed household by 0.21% and

Table 3.11
MPCE by sex-wise head of household

Selected category	*Average MPCE (Rs.) (FE + NFE)*	*Average Per Capita Per Day (Rs.)*	*Share in MPCE by different items*				
			Share of FE		*Share of NFE*		*Village wise % difference with the respective average*
			Average (Rs.)	*(%)*	*Average (Rs.)*	*(%)*	
Male headed household	**945.74**	**31.52**	**718.76**	**76**	**226.98**	**24**	**1**
Longsa	947.77	31.59	691.71	73	256.06	27	+0.21
Yunchuchu	879.81	29.33	668.66	76	211.15	24	-6.97
Sunglup	901.1	30.04	747.91	83	153.19	17	-4.72
Bhandari	1023.02	34.1	859.34	84	163.68	16	+8.17
Female headed household	**924.82**	**30.83**	**730.61**	**79**	**194.21**	**21**	**1**
Longsa	963.29	32.11	770.63	80	192.66	20	+4.16
Yunchuchu	976.61	32.55	712.92	73	263.68	27	+5.6
Sunglup	936.42	31.21	795.95	85	140.47	15	+1.25
Bhandari	658.6	21.95	467.61	71	190.99	29	-28.79

Sources: Field Survey 2005-06.
FE: Food Expenditure.
NFE: Non-food Expenditure.

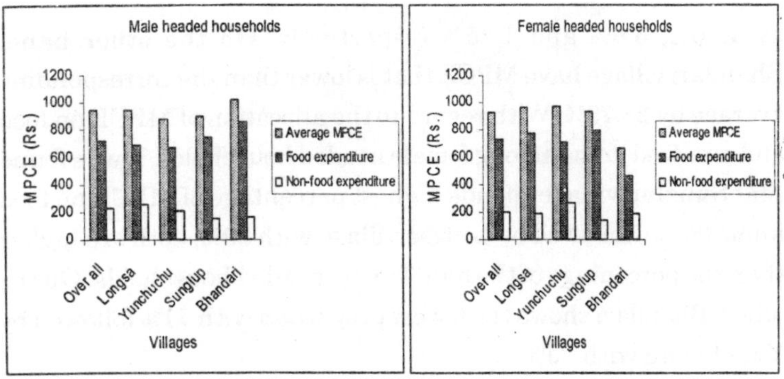

(a) Male headed households MPCE

(b) Female headed households MPCE

Figure 13

8.17% respectively. On the other hand, Sunglup and Yunchuchu villages have MPCE that is lower than the corresponding average by 4.72% and 6.97% respectively. Furthermore, among the male headed households, Bhandari spends highest percentage of MPCE on food items with 84%, followed by Sunglup with 83%; both are higher than the average of the total male headed households of 73%. On the other extreme, Longsa has the lowest percentage with 73%. However, Yunchuchu with 76% is equal to their average.

For the female headed family, the village-wise MPCE are given as follows: Longsa has Rs. 963.29 per month or Rs. 32.11 per person per day at 2005-06 prices, Yunchuchu has Rs. 976.61 per month or Rs. 32.55 per person per day at 2005-06 prices, Sunglup has Rs. 936.42 per month or Rs. 31.21 per person per day at 2005-06 prices and Bhandari has Rs. 658.6 Per Month or Rs. 21.95 per person per day at 2005-06 prices. Among the total female headed households, Longsa, Yunchuchu and Sunglup villages exhibit higher MPCE than the average of total female headed households by 4.16%, 5.6% and 1.25% respectively. On the other hand, Bhandari village have MPCE that is lower than the corresponding average by 28.79%. With regard to the allocation of MPCE on food and non-food items among female headed households, it was found that Sunglup village spends highest percentage of MPCE on food items (85%), followed by Longsa village with 80%; both are higher than the percentage of the total female headed households. On the other, Bhandari shows the lowest proportion with 71% followed by Yunchuchu with 73%.

From the above analysis, it follows that the female headed households in Sunglup and Longsa spend higher proportion of their MPCE on food than male headed households, while in Bhandari and Yunchuchu, male headed household spend higher proportion of their MPCE on food items than female headed households. On an average female headed household spend higher amount of money on food items than male headed household.

4. Decomposition of MPCE by Occupation-wise Head of the Household

The variation in MPCE among the agricultural and service headed households and their allocation pattern and food and non-food items are shown in Table 12 and figure 14 (a) and (b). The average MPCE of agricultural headed households with Rs. 961.12 or 32.04 per person per day at 2005-06 prices is higher than the average sample survey by 1.96%. The corresponding share of food and non- expenditure in MPCE is 78.66% and 21.34% respectively. The village-wise MPCE indicates the following; Longsa has Rs. 959.7 Per Month or Rs. 31.99 per person per day at 2005-06 prices, Yunchuchu has Rs. 878.43 per month or Rs. 29.28 per person per day at 2005-06 prices, Sunglup has Rs. 948.92 per month or Rs. 31.63 per person per day at 2005-06 prices and Bhandari has Rs. 1046.42 per month or Rs. 34.88 per person per day at 2005-06 prices. Among the agricultural headed households, Bhandari village exhibit higher MPCE per month than the average agricultural MPCE by 8.88%. However, Longsa, Sunglup and Yunchuchu villages have MPCE that is lower than the corresponding average by 0.14%, 1.26% and 8.6% respectively. Furthermore, among the agricultural headed households, Bhandari spends highest percentage of MPCE on food items with 85.41%, followed by Yunchuchu with 84.21%, Yunchuchu with 77.15% and Longsa 75.35%. This shows that Longsa village has higher percentage of non-food expenditure in the average MPCE than other villages.

It can be seen from the table and figures that the average MPCE of service headed household is Rs. 999.41 per month or Rs. 33.31 per day per person at 2005-06 prices. The corresponding share of food and non- expenditure in MPCE is 74.46% and 25.54% respectively. The village-wise MPCE indicates the following; Longsa has Rs. 1024.38 per month or Rs. 34.15 per person per day at 2005-06 prices, Yunchuchu has Rs. 977.07 per month or Rs. 32.57 per person per day at 2005-06 prices, Sunglup has Rs. 942.68 per month or Rs. 31.42 per person per day at 2005-06 prices and Bhandari has Rs. 867.12 Per Month or Rs. 28.9 per person per day at 2005-06 prices. Among the villages, Longsa exhibit higher MPCE than the average of the service headed households by 2.49%, while Yunchuchu, Sunglup villages Bhandari village shows a lower MPCE than the corresponding average by 2.2%, 5.68% and 13.24% respectively. Furthermore, in regard to the allocation of MPCE on food and non-food items among service headed households, Sunglup village spends highest percentage of MPCE on food items (80.63%), followed by Sunglup, Yunchuchu and Longsa village with 71.98%, 70.69% and 70.55% respectively.

Table 3.12
MPCE by Occupation-wise Head of Household

Selected category	*Average MPCE (Rs.) (FE + NFE)*	*Average Per Capita Per Day (Rs.)*	*Share in MPCE by different items*				
			Share of FE		*Share of NFE*		*Village wise % difference with the respective average*
			Average (Rs.)	*(%)*	*Average (Rs.)*	*(%)*	
Agricultural headed household	**961.12**	**32.04**	**756.02**	**78.66**	**205.1**	**21.34**	**1**
Longsa	959.7	31.99	723.13	75.35	236.57	24.65	-.14
Yunchuchu	878.43	29.28	677.71	77.15	200.72	22.85	-.8.6
Sunglup	948.92	31.63	799.09	84.21	149.83	15.79	-1.26
Bhandari	1046.42	34.88	893.75	85.41	152.67	14.59	+8.88
Service headed household	**999.41**	**33.31**	**744.16**	**74.46**	**255.25**	**25.54**	**1**
Longsa	1024.38	34.15	722.7	70.55	301.68	29.45	+2.49
Yunchuchu	977.07	32.57	690.69	70.69	286.38	29.31	-2.2
Sunglup	942.68	31.42	678.54	71.98	264.14	28.02	-5.68
Bhandari	867.12	28.9	699.16	80.63	167.96	19.37	-13.24

Sources: Field Survey 2005-06.
FE: Food Expenditure.
NFE: Non-food Expenditure.

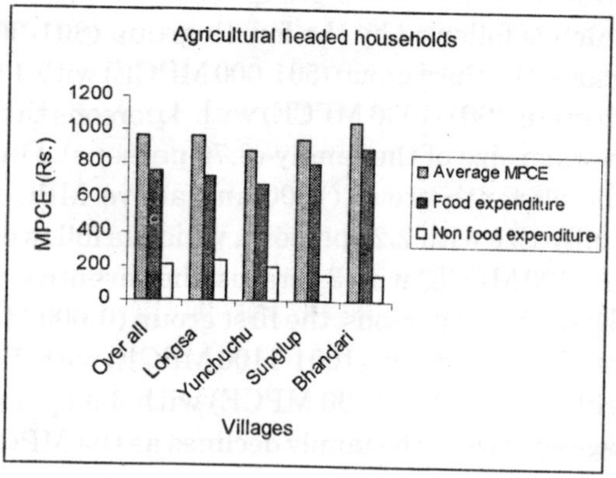

Figure 14 (a) Agricultural headed household MPCE

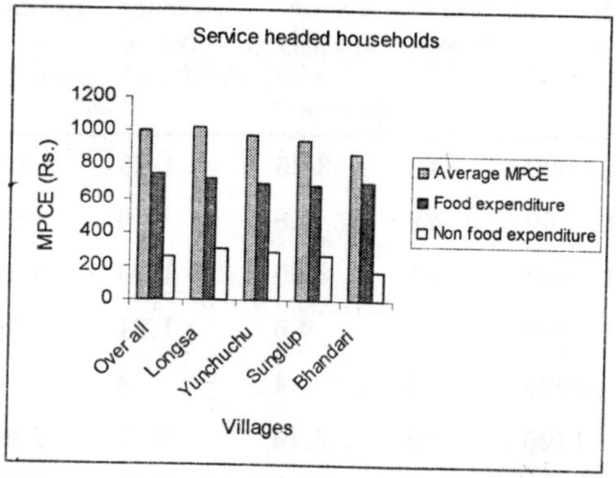

Figure 14 (b) Service headed household MPCE

5. MPCE and family size

Table 3.13 and figure 15 given below explains the relationship between MPCE and the size of family. It is shown here in the table that the size of family decreases as the average MPCE increases, giving us an inverse relation between the two. Table 3.13 and figure 15 shows that the size of the family fluctuates across MPCE groups. By MPCE groups, the average size of the family is largest in the second group (601-700 MPCE) with 5.8 persons, which is followed by the fourth group (801-900 MPCE) with 4.5 persons, the third group (501-600 MPCE) with 4.35 persons and the fifth group (901-1000 MPCE) with 4 persons that is higher than the average size of the family (3.76 persons). On the other extreme, the eleventh group (1500 and above MPCE) has the smallest family size with 2.25 persons, which is followed by ninth group (1301-1400 MPCE) with 3 persons, the seventh group (1101-1200 MPCE) with 3.13 persons, the first group (0-600 MPCE) with 3.25 persons, the sixth group (1001-1100 MPCE) with 3.46 persons and the eight group (1201-1300 MPCE) with 3.63 persons. Thus on an average the size of the family declines as the MPCE goes up.

Table 3.13
MPCE and family size

No of House-holds	*MPCE group (Rs.)*	*No of Persons*	*Average family size (persons)*	*Average No. of children**	*average no. of adult***	*Average MPCE (Rs.)*
4	0 – 600	13	3.25	1.75	1.5	526.99
5	601 - 700	29	5.8	1.6	4.2	652.31
14	701 - 800	61	4.35	1.93	2.42	745.94
26	801 - 900	117	4.5	1.81	2.69	842.92
10	901 - 1000	40	4	3	1	946.36
13	1001 - 1100	45	3.46	0.77	2.69	1067.39
8	1101 - 1200	25	3.13	0.25	2.88	1149.87
8	1201 - 1300	29	3.63	0.5	3.13	1240.11
3	1301 - 1400	9	3	1	2	1329.57
4	1401 - 1500	16	4	1.75	2.25	1429.49
5	1500 and above	9	2.25	0.25	2	1429.49

Sources: Field Survey 2005-06.
* Persons under 15 years of age.
** Persons 15 years and above.

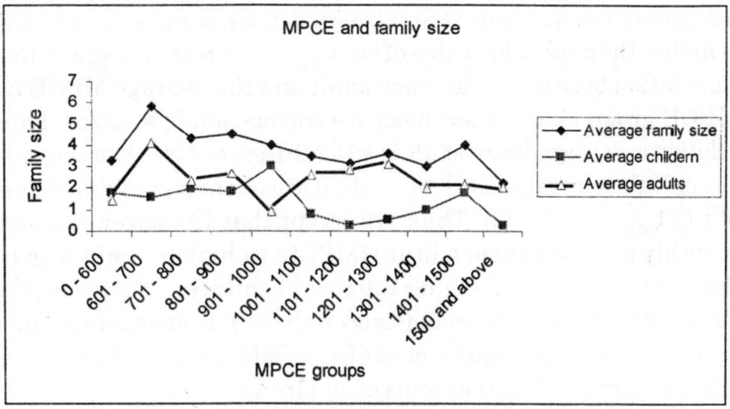

Figure 15: MPCE and family size

This relationship can be ascertained by looking at the correlation between the two variables.

r = -0.57

Thus from the correlation (r) between the two, it shows that there is an inverse relation between family size and the MPCE. It means that smaller the size of the family, higher is the expenditure on food and non-food items. To find whether the correlation coefficient is significant at 5% level, t-test for the given distribution is done. The calculated value of t comes out to be $|t| = 2.08$ whereas the table value $|t_{0.05}| = 1.833$. Since the calculated value is higher than the table value, the correlation is significant at 5% level for 9 degrees of freedom. Therefore, the hypothesis is accepted. Hence higher the family size lower will be the MPCE.

The reason why smaller family size requires higher expenditure can be explained by taking the number of children in each MPCE group into consideration. It can be seen that on an average the number of children goes on decreasing as the average MPCE goes on increasing. By looking at the correlation between the average number of children and the average MPCE in MPCE group, it was found that there exist a negative correlation (r = -.523). This negative correlation is significant at 5% level for

9 degree of freedom since the calculated value of t ($|t| = 1.8435$) is higher than the table value of t ($|t_{0.05}| = 1.833$). However, the correlation between an average adult and the average MPCE in MPCE group shows a low negative correlation (r = -.325). This relation is not significant at 5% level for 9 degree of freedom because the calculated value of t ($|t| = .325$) is less than the table value of t ($|t_{0.05}| = 1.833$). Thus, we accept that the lower average monthly per capita expenditure (MPCE) in higher family size is due to the presence of higher number of children. The reason is that under any normal circumstances, the requirement of an adult cost more than the requirement of any children, *e.g.*, cloths of an adult cost more than the cloths of children.

To measure the effect on MPCE from a change in family size has been analysed through simple regression method. Regression equation of Y on X is; Y-Mean of Y = byx (X- Mean of X)

$$Y = 1755.163 - 192.08X$$

Where, y is the monthly per capita expenditure (MPCE) and x is the family size. This result shows that the regression coefficient 'byx' of Y on X is -192.08. The negative value of the regression coefficient indicates that the relation between y and x is indirect. This shows that a unit change in the family size (X) will have an impact on MPCE of the people (Y) by -192.08 times. To see whether the regression analysis is significant or not, t-test is undertaken. The result shows that the calculated value of t ($|t| = 64.89$) is much higher than the table value ($|t_{0.05}| = 1.833$), therefore, the value of b is significant at 5% level for 9 degrees of freedom. Hence a small change in family size will have a large negative impact on MPCE.

6. MPCE and Average Calorie Intake

Since MPCE is the best measure of poverty than income as provided from the data, it is important to examine the relationship between the MPCE and average calorie intake per day. The MPCE is used as a proxy of income.

Table 3.14
Average calorie intake and MPCE

Sl. No	*MPCE group (Rs.)*	*Average MPCE (Rs.)*	*Average calorie (Kcal)*
1	0 - 600	526.99	1826.27
2	601 - 700	652.31	1950.71
3	701 - 800	745.94	2139.71
4	801 - 900	842.92	2154.46
5	901 - 1000	946.36	2711.33
6	1001 - 1100	1067.39	2884.94
7	1101 - 1200	1149.87	2898.11
8	1201 - 1300	1240.11	3151.26
9	1301 - 1400	1329.57	3443.7
10	1401 - 1500	1429.49	2931.2
11	1501 and above	1429.49	3338.92

Sources: Field Survey 2005-06.

The data on MPCE and average calorie intake per day are shown in Table 3.14 and figure 16. Here one could clearly see that as the level of MPCE goes up, the average calorie intake also increases in the same direction. The data in the table and figure shows that the lowest MPCE group are having a per capita consumption of calorie at 1826.27 Kcal per day, for the second MPCE group it is 1950.71 Kcal per capita per day, the third MPCE group have 2139.71 Kcal per capita per day, for the fourth MPCE group it is 2154.71 Kcal per capita per day, for the fifth MPCE group it is 2711.33 Kcal per capita per day, for the sixth MPCE group it is 2884.94 Kcal per capita per day, for the seventh MPCE group it is 2898.11 Kcal per capita per day, for the eighth MPCE group it is 3151.26 Kcal per capita per day, for the ninth MPCE group it is 3443.7 Kcal per capita per day, for the tenth MPCE group it is 2931.2 Kcal per person per day and for the highest MPCE group (eleven group) it is 3338.92 Kcal per person per day. Thus from the average it can be seen that the average calorie intake goes on increasing along with the MPCE group till the ninth MPCE group. Then there is a slight fall in per capita calorie intake in the tenth MPCE group. But in general the per capita calorie intake shows a rising trend as the MPCE group goes up. This means that higher the MPCE, higher is the calorie intake per person. Thus, there is a positive relation between MPCE and per capita calorie intake. So the proposition that higher the income, higher is the calorie intake appears to be true once we take MPCE as the real income of the people.

To examine the relationship between monthly MPCE and average calorie intake per day, their correlation coefficient (r) have been worked out as follows,

$r = 0.94$

This implies that there is a high positive relationship between per capita monthly expenditure and per capita calorie intake. In other words, people with higher MPCE take more calories. To find whether the correlation coefficient is significant at 5% level, t-test for the given distribution is calculated. The calculated value of t comes out to be $t = 23.5$ whereas the table value $t_{0.05} = 1.833$. Since the calculated value is much higher than the table value, the correlation is significant at 5% level for 9 degrees of freedom. Therefore, the hypothesis is accepted. Hence people with higher monthly MPCE consumes higher calorie.

To measure the effect on per capita calorie intake from a change in monthly MPCE has been analysed through simple regression method. Regression equation of Y on X is; Y-Mean of Y = byx(X-Mean of X)

$Y = 919.81 + 1.7X.$

Where, y is the per capita calorie intake per day and x is the monthly per capita expenditure (MPCE). This result shows that the regression coefficient 'byx' of Y on X is 1.7. The positive value of the regression coefficient indicates that the relation between y and x is direct. This shows that a unit change in the MPCE (X) will have an impact on per capita calorie intake of the people (Y) by 1.7 times. To see whether the regression analysis is significant or not, t-test is undertaken. The result shows that the calculated value of t (t = 8.401) is much higher than the table value ($t_{0.05}$ = 1.833), therefore, the value of b is significant at 5% level for 9 degrees of freedom. Hence a small change in monthly MPCE will have a positive impact on calorie intake of the people.

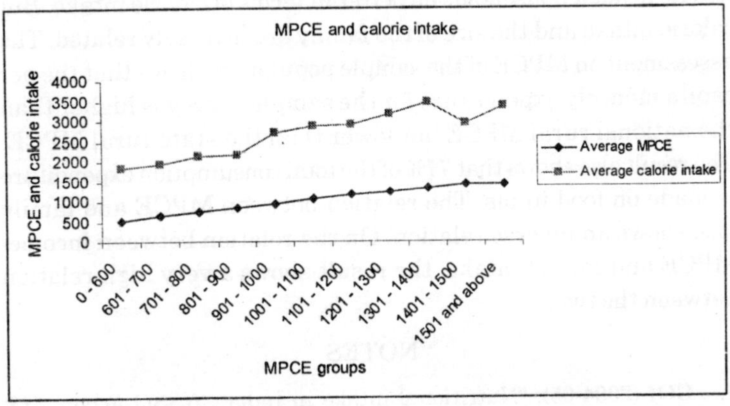

Figure 16: MPCE and Calorie intake

The regression line is shown by figure 17.

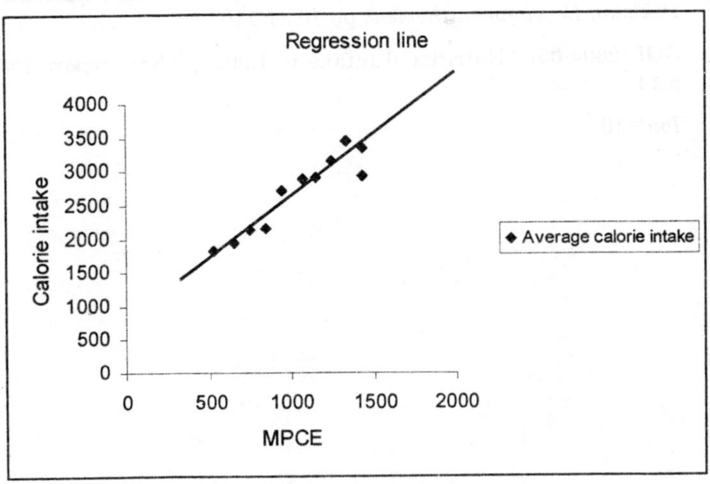

Figure 17: Regression line of average MPCE and calorie intake

In conclusion, we see that the average sample population calorie intake is higher than the rural calorie norms of the State and Nation. The assessment on calorie intake also shows that on an average the calorie intake rose with the age. However, sex-wise calorie intake shows that female calorie intake is higher on an average. Among the heads of family by sex, it is shown that female headed households do better in terms of calorie intake. But calorie intake and the size of the family are inversely related. The assessment on MPCE of the sample population shows that the per capita monthly expenditure for the sample survey is higher than the national rural MPCE but lower than the state rural MPCE. The result also shows that 77% of the total consumption expenditure is made on food items. The relation between MPCE and family size shows an inverse relation. On the relation between income/ MPCE and calorie intake, the result shows a very high relation between the two.

NOTES

1. GOI (2004-05), "Nutritional intake in India", *NSSO Report 513*, p i.
2. Pradhan, B. K., and Saluja, M.R., (1998), 'An Assessment of Poverty Studies in India with Special Reference to Economic Reforms', *Pakistan Development Review*, pp.10 81-1102.
3. GOI (2004-05), "Nutritional intake in India". *NSSO report 508*, p.14.
4. *Ibid.* 10.

4

Measuring Poverty

In the previous chapter, the assessments of nutritional intake and MPCE have been discussed in detailed. In this section the extent and depth of poverty among the sample population has been estimated using nutritional norms and MPCE. A comparative analysis on poverty between the norms set by NSSO and sample norms has also been thoroughly discussed here in this section. Moreover, this section also highlights the impact of poverty alleviation programme on the sample population.

Poverty Line and Nutritional Norms

Poverty line serves as a cut-off line for separating the poor from non-poor. In India, the derivation of the minimum normative absolute living standard or poverty line is based on the calorific norms and per capita monthly expenditure (MPCE). The national aggregate daily calorie requirement is calculated by summing up the nutritional intake across all individuals. The average calorie intake is then calculated by dividing the national aggregate of daily calorie intake with the total population. Thus, the minimum nutritional norm for the sample population is arrived at by calculating the average calorie intake of the entire individual. Then, the cost/expenditure of the normative calorie requirement is worked out, which yield a poverty norm that could be called starvation line or food energy requirement.[1] However, in deriving the poverty line, the average expenditure of the households on both food and non-food items are calculated. To convert this to per capita amount, the household expenditure on food and non-food items are divided by the number of person in each household, this gives the monthly per capita total expenditure, or the MPCE or the poverty norms. The nutritional norms of the sample survey and the NSSO estimate is given in the Tables 4.1 (a) while the estimated poverty line of the sample survey and the NSSO is given in the Table 4.1 (b). From the Table 4.1 (a) it is evident that the per capita calorie intake fixed by the NSSO at the National level is 2047 is higher than the State level of 2044 but lower than the sample estimate by 394.92 Kcal in the rural areas.

Table 4.1 (a)
Calorie Norms

Group	*Calorie Intake Per day (Kcal) Rural areas*
*National (2004-05)	2047
*Nagaland State (2004-05)	2044
Sample Estimate (2005-06)	2441.92

Source: * NSSO, report 513 and Field Survey 2005-06.

The NSSO and the Sample survey estimates of Poverty line for rural areas based on MPCE are given in the Table 4.1 (b).

Table 4.1 (b)
Poverty line/MPCE

Group	*MPCE (Rs.) for Rural areas*	*Per Capita per Day (Rs.)*
*National 2004-05 (At 2004-05 prices)	558.78	18.63
*State 2004-05 (At 2004-05 prices)	1010.81	33.69
From the estimate for 2005-06 (At 2005-06 prices)	942.60	31.41

Source: *NSSO, report 508 and Field Survey 2005-06.

From the table it is clear that the NSSO estimates of Nagaland MPCE is higher than the National level MPCE. That is, Nagaland poverty line has been fixed at Rs. 1010.81 per person per month or Rs. 33.69 per person per day at 2004-05 prices and national level is Rs. 558.78 per person per month or Rs. 18.63 per person per day at 2004-05 prices. However, the sample survey estimate shows an MPCE of Rs. 942.66 per person per month or Rs. 31.42 per person per day at 2005-06 prices, which is lower than the State level but higher than the National level.

Extent and Depth of Poverty

From the sample data poverty has been measured at village level, gender-wise, sex-wise head of the family and occupation-wise head of the households in the rural area using both calorific norms and the MPCE or the poverty line. The extent of absolute poverty is measured using tools such as Head Count Ratio, Poverty Gap Ratio, Foster Greer and Thorbecke and Sen Index.

1. Measuring Poverty through Calorie Intake

The rural average calorie norms of NSSO 61st round for the Nation and State and the Sample survey average are used to measure the calorie deprivation among the sample population. The resultant figures of the analysis are given in Table 4.2.

(a) Sample Population

From the Table 4.2 it is seen that Head Count Ratio (HCR) based on 2047 Kcal and 2044 Kcal cutoff are the same and is 28.75%. This means that 28.75% of the sample population are poor or are living below the calorie norms. Whereas, the HCR based on 2441.92 Kcal cutoffs shows a higher percentage of poor for the sample population with 46.06%. This percentage of poor is higher than the number of poor estimated using the National and State calorie norms by 17.57%.

The calorie gap ratio based on 2047 Kcal is 10.01% per poor person for the sample population. This means that every poor person is falling short of the calorie norm by 204.9 Kcal. In other words, to support every poor person at the calorie requirement level, 204.9 of calorie intake is needed per poor person. However, calorie gap ratio based on 2044 Kcal cutoff shows a lower percentage

Table 4.2
Measuring Poverty through Calorie Norms

Category	Head Count Ratio (HCR)			Poverty Gap (PG)			Sen Index (P)			Foster, Greer and Thorbecke (P^F)		
	1	*2*	*3*	*1*	*2*	*3*	*1*	*2*	*3*	*1*	*2*	*3*
Sample population	.2875	.2875	.4606	.1001	.0997	.1449	.0765	.0764	.1159	.0592	.0591	.0779
Gender-wise												
Male	.3081	.3081	.4826	.1010	.1007	.1563	.0801	.0799	.1240	.0582	.0581	.0839
Female	.2805	.2805	.4479	.0986	.0984	.1405	.0789	.0787	.1124	.0605	.0604	.0778
Village-wise												
Longsa	.2973	.2973	.4633	.1060	.1057	.1534	.0846	.0844	.1209	.0651	.0650	.0861
Yunchuchu	.2857	.2857	.5476	.1338	.1336	.1744	.1039	.1037	.1354	.0790	.0789	.1008
Sunglup	.2105	.2105	.2895	.0457	.0455	.0762	.0577	.0575	.0687	.0160	.0159	.0305
Bhandari	.3148	.3148	.4815	.0720	.0717	.1293	.0586	.0584	.1006	.0351	.0350	.0546
Range-wise												
Upper	.2973	.2973	.4633	.1060	.1057	.1534	.0846	.0844	.1209	.0651	.0650	.0861
Middle	.25	.25	.45	.0918	.0916	.1274	.1197	.1195	.1852	.0498	.0496	.0674
Lower	.3148	.3148	.4815	.0720	.0717	.1293	.0586	.0584	.1006	.0351	.0350	.0546

(Contd...)

Sex-wise head of household												
Male headed family	.3035	.3035	.4601	.1202	.1111	.1558	0834	.0832	.1228	.0667	.0665	.0865
Female headed family	.1875	.1875	.4375	. 0569	. 0568	.1009	.0475	.0473	.0842	.0306	.0305	.0446
Occupation-wise head of household												
Service	.2704	.2704	.4654	.0823	.0821	.1296	.0701	.0698	.1104	.0442	.0441	.0888
Agricultural	.3034	.3034	.4531	.1127	.1124	.1550	.0878	.0876	.1209	.0696	.0694	.0886

Source: Field survey 2005-06

1 – Calorie Norms of 2047 Kcal per person per day (National Norms)

2 – Calorie Norms of 2044 Kcal per person per day (State Norms)

3 – Calorie Norms of 2441.92 Kcal per person per day (Sample Survey Norms)

of 9.97% per poor person for the sample population. This means that every poor person is falling short of the calorie norm by 203.79 Kcal. Whereas, the calorie gap ratio based on 2441.92 Kcal cutoffs shows a higher calorie deprivation for the sample population with 14.49% per poor person. It means to support every poor person at the calorie norms, calorie intake of 353.83 Kcal per poor person is required. Thus, calorie gap ratio based on 2441.92 Kcal shows a deeper calorie deprivation than the calorie gap ratio based on National and State norms by about (151 Kcal) 4.48% per poor person.

Sen Index (P) based on 2047 Kcal is 7.65% for the sample population. This means that 7.65% of poor amongst the poor are falling below their average calorie norm. Whereas, Sen Index based on 2044 Kcal cutoff shows that 7.64% of poorest amongst the poor are falling below their average calorie norm. However, the P based on 2441.92 Kcal cutoffs shows a higher extent of calorie deprivation with 11.59% of poorest amongst the poor falling below their calorie norm. Thus, P based on 2441.92 Kcal shows a higher percentage of poorest amongst the poor than the P based on national and state norms by about 3.95%.

The estimation of Foster, Greer and Thorbecke (P^F) based on 2047 Kcal cutoff reveals that the severity of calorie deprivation among the sample population is 5.92% for the poorest among the poor. This means that 5.92% of the poorest among the poor are far below the calorie norms. In other words, the severity of calorie inadequacy falls on 5.92% of the poorest poor among the sample population. The analysis of P^F based on 2044 Kcal cutoff shows that 5.91% of the poorest among the poor are far below the calorie norms. However, the P^F based on 2441.92 Kcal cutoff shows that calorie inadequacy is more severe with 7.79%. It means 7.79% of the poorest poor among the sample population are far below the calorie norms. Thus, P^F based on 2441.92 Kcal shows a more severity in calorie inadequacy than the P^F based on national and state norms by about 2.37% for the poorest poor.

(b) Gender-wise

The Gender-wise analysis of HCR base on 2047 Kcal and 2044 Kcal cutoff shows that, male (30.81%) have a higher percentage of poor than female (28.05%) by 2.76%. The estimation of HCR using 2441.92 Kcal cutoff shows that the percentage of poor for male is 48.26% while for female; it is 44.79% of poor population.

Calorie gap ratio estimates based on 2047 Kcal for male and female shows that male have higher ratio of 10.10% than female ratio of 9.86%. It means that to place every poor person at the calorie norms, calorie intake of 206.75 Kcal per poor person and 201.83 Kcal per poor person respectively, is required by male and female poor population. However, calorie gap ratio based on 2044 Kcal cutoff shows a lower percentage for both male and female population. The figures in the table show that male calorie gap is (205.83 Kcal) 10.07% per poor person and female calorie gap is (201.12 Kcal) 9.84% per poor person. Whereas, the calorie gap ratio based on 2441.92 Kcal cutoff shows a higher calorie deprivation for both male and female population with 15.63% and 14.05% per poor person respectively. On comparison between male and female calorie gap ratio based on different calorie norms, it is seen from the table that the calorie gap ratio of male is higher than female across different calorie norms.

Gender-wise Sen Index based on 2047 Kcal shows that male have higher percentage of poor amongst the poor than female. The result of the analysis shows that male has 8.01% of poor amongst the poor falling below their calorie norm, while female have 7.89% of poor amongst the poor falling below their calorie norm. The estimation of P based on 2044 Kcal cutoff shows a similar result with small difference. The figure in the table indicates that male have 7.99% of poor amongst the poor whose calorie intake are falling below their calorie norm that is slightly higher than female percentage of 7.87%. However, P based on 2441.92 Kcal cutoff shows that male population have 12.40% of poor amongst the poor falling below their calorie norm, while female have 11.24% of poor amongst the poor falling below their calorie norm. The comparison between male and female Sen Index based on different calorie norms show that Sen Index of male is higher than female across different calorie norms.

The estimation of Foster, Greer and Thorbecke (P^F) based on 2047 Kcal shows that gender-wise calorie deprivation is more severe for female population than male population. The result of the analysis shows that the severity of calorie inadequacy falls on 6.05 % of the poorest poor for female population, while it is 5.82% of the poorest poor for male population. The estimation of P^F based on 2044 Kcal shows that, calorie inadequacy for both male and female is 5.81% and 6.04% of the poorest poor respectively. However, P^F based on 2441.92 Kcal cutoff shows a higher calorie inadequacy than the result based on National and State calorie norms. It can be seen from the table that severity of calorie inadequacy falls on 8.39% of the poorest poor for male population, while it is 7.78% for the female population. The comparison between male and female P^F based on different calorie norms show that the severity of calorie inadequacy for female is higher than male at lower calorie norms calorie norms but lower at the higher calorie norms.

(c) Village-wise

The village-wise HCR estimate based on 2047 Kcal and 2044 Kcal cutoff shows that, Bhandari has the highest percentage of poor with 31.48%, followed by Longsa with 29.73% and Yunchuchu with 28.57%. Sunglup with 21.05% exhibits the lowest percentage of poor. However, the estimation of HCR based on 2441.92 Kcal cutoffs indicates a higher proportion of poor among the sample population. Among the villages, Yunchuchu with 54.76% has the highest proportion of population living below the calorie norms. This is followed Bhandari with 48.15% and Longsa with 46.33%. Sunglup shows the lowest proportion of poor with 28.95%. The use of different calorie norms influences the magnitude of head count ratio. On an average, HCR based on 2441.92 Kcal cutoff are higher by 17.57% than HCR computed using 2047 Kcal and 2044 Kcal. It may be noted that, among the villages, Bhandari exhibits the highest percentage of poor when measured using National and State calorie norms. However, using the sample calorie norms, it is found that Yunchuchu has the highest percentage of poor.

The estimation of calorie gap ratio based on 2047 Kcal cutoff shows that, among the villages, the depth of calorie deprivation is highest in Yunchuchu with (273.89 Kcal) 13.38% per poor person, this followed by Longsa with (216.98 Kcal) 10.6% per poor person and Bhandari with (147.38 Kcal) 7.20% per poor person. Sunglup with (93.55 Kcal) 4.57% per poor person exhibits the lowest calorie deprivation among the villages. The calorie gap ratio estimates based on 2044 Kcal cutoff shows similar result to that of the analysis based 2047 calorie norms but lower ratio. It can be seen from the table that the depth of calorie deprivation is highest in Yunchuchu with (273.09 Kcal) 13.36% per poor person, followed by Longsa with (216.05 Kcal) 10.57% per poor person and Bhandari with (147.17 Kcal) 7.17% per poor person. Sunglup with (93 Kcal) 4.55% per poor person exhibits the lowest calorie deprivation among the villages. However, the estimation of calorie gap ratio based on 2441.92 Kcal cutoffs indicates a higher calorie deprivation among the sample population. Among the villages, Yunchuchu with (433.19 Kcal) 17.44% per poor person shows the highest shortfall of calorie norms. This is followed by Longsa with (374.59 Kcal) 15.34% per poor person and Bhandari with (315.74 Kcal) 12.93% per poor person. Sunglup with (186.07 Kcal) 7.62% shows the lowest calorie deprivation among the villages. On comparison among different villages calorie gap ratio based on different calorie norms, it is seen from the table that the calorie gap ratio of Yunchuchu is higher than other villages across different calorie norms, while Sunglup exhibits lower gap than other villages.

The analysis of Sen Index (P) based on 2047 Kcal cutoff shows that, Yunchuchu with 10.39% exhibits the highest percentage of poor amongst the poor falling below their calorie norm. It is followed by Longsa with 8.46% and Bhandari with 5.86% of poor amongst the poor falling below their calorie norm. Sunglup with 5.77% of poor amongst the poor falling below their calorie norm exhibits the lowest percentage among the villages. The P estimates based on 2044 Kcal cutoff shows similar result to that of the analysis based 2047 calorie norms with small difference. It can be seen from the table that the extent of calorie deprivation is highest in Yunchuchu with 10.37% of poor amongst the poor falling below their calorie norm. It is followed by Longsa with 8.44% and Bhandari with 5.84% of poor amongst the poor falling below their calorie norm. Sunglup with 5.75% of poor amongst the poor falling below their calorie norm exhibits the lowest percentage among the villages. However, the estimation of P based on 2441.92 Kcal cutoffs indicates a higher percentage of poor amongst the poor falling below their calorie norm for the sample population. Among the villages, Yunchuchu with 13.54% have the highest percentage of poor amongst the poor falling below their calorie norm. This is followed by Longsa with 12.09% and Bhandari with 10.06% of poor amongst the poor falling below their calorie norm. Sunglup with 6.87% of poor amongst the poor falling below their calorie norm shows the lowest percentage among the villages. On comparison among different villages Sen Index based on different calorie norms, it is seen from the table that Sen Index of Yunchuchu is higher than other villages across different calorie norms, while Sunglup exhibits smaller Sen Index than other villages.

Estimation of Foster, Greer and Thorbecke (P^F) based on 2047 Kcal cutoff shows that, the calorie inadequacy is more severe in Yunchuchu with 7.9% for the poorest poor. It means 7.9% of the poorest poor in Yunchuchu are far below the calorie norm. It is followed by Longsa with 6.51% and Bhandari with 3.51% of the poorest poor facing calorie inadequacy. Sunglup with 1.6% of the poorest poor facing calorie inadequacy exhibits the lowest severity of calorie deprivation among the villages. The P^F estimates based on 2044 Kcal cutoff shows a similar result to that of the analysis based 2047 calorie norms with small difference. It can be seen from the table that the severity of calorie deprivation is highest in Yunchuchu with 7.89% for the poorest poor. It is followed by Longsa with 6.50% and Bhandari with 3.50% of the poorest poor facing calorie inadequacy. Sunglup with 1.59% of the poorest poor facing calorie inadequacy exhibits the lowest severity of calorie deprivation among the villages. However, the estimation of P^F based on 2441.92

Kcal cutoffs indicates a higher severity of calorie deprivation among the sample villages. Among the villages, Yunchuchu with 10.08% of the poorest poor shows the highest percentage of severity in calorie deprivation. This is followed by Longsa with 8.61% and Bhandari with 5.46% of the poorest poor facing calorie inadequacy. Sunglup with 3.05% of the poorest poor facing calorie inadequacy shows the lowest severity in calorie deprivation among the villages. Comparison of the severity in calorie deprivation among different villages based on different calorie norms shows that Yunchuchu has higher inadequacy than other villages across different calorie norms, while Sunglup exhibits smaller calorie inadequacy than other villages.

(d) Range-wise

Range-wise estimation of poverty is shown in the Table 4.2. From the table it is clear that the upper range is represented by Longsa village and lower range is represented by Bhandari village. Thus, the explanation given for these villages also represents their respective range. However, middle range is represented by two villages, viz, Yunchuchu and Sunglup.

The range-wise HCR estimate based on 2047 Kcal and 2044 Kcal cutoff shows that, middle range has the lowest percentage of poor with 25%. However, the estimation of HCR based on 2441.92 Kcal cutoffs indicates a higher proportion of poor among the sample ranges. Among the ranges, lower range with 48.15% has the highest proportion of population living below the calorie norms, while middle range with 45% of the people living below their calorie norms has the lowest percentage of poor. On comparison among different ranges HCR based on different calorie norms, it is seen from the table that middle range has the highest proportion of poor among the ranges.

The estimation of calorie gap ratio based on 2047 Kcal cutoff shows that, among the ranges, the depth of calorie deprivation is highest in upper range with (216.98 Kcal) 10.6% per poor person followed by middle range with (187.63) 9.18%. Lower range with (147.38 Kcal) 7.20% per poor person exhibits the lowest calorie deprivation among the ranges. The calorie gap ratio estimates based on 2044 Kcal cutoff shows similar result to that of the analysis based 2047 calorie norms but lower ratio. It can be seen from the table that the depth of calorie deprivation is highest in upper range with (216.05 Kcal) 10.57% per poor person followed by middle range with (187.23) 9.16%. Lower range with (147.17 Kcal) 7.17% per poor person exhibits the lowest calorie deprivation among the ranges. However, the estimation of calorie gap ratio based on 2441.92 Kcal cutoffs indicates a higher calorie deprivation among the sample ranges. Among the ranges, upper range with (374.59 Kcal) 15.34% per poor person has the highest calorie deprivation, while middle range with (311.1) 12.74% shows the lowest calorie deprivation among the ranges. On comparison among different ranges calorie gap ratio based on different calorie norms, it is seen from the table that the calorie gap ratio of upper range is higher than other ranges across different calorie norms.

The analysis of Sen Index (P) based on 2047 Kcal cutoff shows that, middle range with 11.97% exhibits the highest percentage of poor amongst the poor falling below their calorie norm. Lower range with 5.86% of poor amongst the poor falling below their calorie norm exhibits the lowest percentage among the ranges. The P estimates based on 2044 Kcal cutoff shows similar result to that of the analysis based 2047 calorie norms with small difference. It can be seen from the table that the extent of calorie deprivation is highest in middle range with 11.95% of poor amongst the poor falling below their calorie norm. Lower range with 5.84% of poor amongst the poor falling below their calorie norm exhibits the lowest percentage among the ranges. However, the estimation of P based on 2441.92 Kcal cutoffs indicates a higher percentage of poor amongst the poor falling below their calorie norm for the sample ranges. Among the ranges, middle range with 18.52% has the highest percentage of poor amongst the poor falling below their calorie noım. Lower range with 10.06% of poor amongst the poor falling below their calorie norm shows the lowest percentage among the ranges. On comparison among different ranges Sen Index based on different calorie norms, it is seen from the table that Sen Index of middle range is higher than other ranges across different calorie norms.

Estimation of Foster, Greer and Thorbecke (P^F) based on 2047 Kcal cutoff shows that, the calorie inadequacy is more severe in upper range with 6.51% of the poorest poor facing calorie inadequacy. It is followed by middle range with 4.99% and lower range with 3.51% of the poorest poor facing calorie inadequacy. The P^F estimates based on 2044 Kcal cutoff shows a similar result to that of the analysis based 2047 calorie norms with small difference. It can be seen from the table that the severity of calorie deprivation is highest upper range with 6.50%. It is followed by middle range with 4.97% and lower range with 3.50% of the poorest poor facing calorie inadequacy. However, the estimation of P^F based on 2441.92 Kcal cutoffs indicates a higher severity of calorie deprivation among the sample ranges. Among the ranges, upper range with 8.61% of the poorest poor shows the highest percentage of severity in calorie deprivation. This is followed by middle range with 6.74% and lower range with 5.46% of the poorest poor facing calorie inadequacy. Comparing the severity in calorie deprivation among different ranges based on different calorie norms shows that upper range has higher inadequacy than other ranges across different calorie norms, while lower range exhibits smaller calorie inadequacy than other ranges.

(e) Sex-wise head of household

Sex-wise head of household estimation of HCR based on 2047 Kcal and 2044 Kcal cutoff shows that the proportion of poor is higher in male headed family than female headed family. The table shows that 30.35% of the population in male headed family is below the calorie norms, while female headed family has 18.75% of poor people. The estimation of HCR using 2441.92 Kcal cutoff shows an increase in magnitude of poor but lesser difference in the proportion of poor between male and female headed family. The proportion of poor for male headed family is 46.01%, while it is 43.75% for the female headed family. Thus, it is clear that male headed family have higher proportion of poor across different calorie norms.

The analysis of calorie gap ratio based on 2047 Kcal cutoff shows that the depth of calorie deprivation is higher in male headed family than female headed family. Table No. 4.2 shows that the depth of calorie deprivation in male headed family is 12.02% per poor person, while it is 5.69% per poor person for female headed family. It means to help every poor person at the calorie norms, calorie intake of 246.05 Kcal and 116.47 Kcal per person is required by the poor population of male headed family and female headed family respectively. However, calorie gap ratio based on 2044 Kcal cutoff shows a lower percentage for both male and female headed family. The figures in the table shows that male headed households has calorie gap of (227.09 Kcal) 11.11% per poor person while it is (116.09 Kcal) 5.68% per poor person for female headed households. The estimation of calorie gap ratio using 2441.92 Kcal cutoff shows an increase in the depth of calorie deprivation in both male and female headed family. The calorie short fall of the population in male headed family is 15.58% per poor person, while it is 10.09% per poor person in female headed family. On comparison between male and female headed calorie gap ratio based on different calorie norms, it can be seen that calorie gap ratio of male headed household is higher than female headed household.

Estimation of P based on 2047 Kcal cutoff shows that the percentage of poor amongst the poor falling below their calorie norm in male headed family is 8.34%, while it is 4.75% for the female headed family. Sen Index based on 2044 Kcal cutoff shows that male headed households has 8.32% of poor amongst the poor falling below their calorie norm, while it is 4.73% female headed households. However, Sen Index based on 2441.92 Kcal cutoff shows that the percentage of poor amongst the poor falling below their calorie norm in male headed family is 12.28%, while it is 8.42% for the female headed family. On comparison between male and female headed Sen Index based on different calorie norms, it can be seen that Sen Index of male headed household is higher than female headed households.

The estimation of P^F based on 2047 Kcal cutoff shows that the severity of calorie deprivation in male headed family is 6.67% for the poorest poor, while it is 3.06% for the poorest poor of the female headed family. The result of P^F based on 2044 Kcal cutoff shows similar result with 6.65% of the poorest poor facing calorie deficiency by male headed family, while 3.05% of the poorest poor in female headed family are facing calorie deficiency. However, the estimation of calorie inadequacy using 2441.92 Kcal cutoff shows an increase in the severity of calorie deprivation in both male and female headed family. The calorie inadequacy in male headed family is 8.65% for the poorest poor, while it is 4.46% for the poorest poor in female headed family. On comparison between male and female headed family P^F based on different calorie norms, it was found that calorie deficiency is higher in male headed family than female headed family.

(f) Occupation-wise head of household

The estimation of HCR based on 2047 Kcal and 2044 Kcal cutoff shows that the proportion of poor is higher in the household headed by agriculturalist than the services. From the table it is seen that the household headed by agriculturalist have 30.34% of its population below the calorie norms, whereas, those household headed by service have 27.04% of its population below the calorie norm. However, the estimation of HCR based on 2441.92 Kcal cutoffs indicates that the service headed family has higher proportion of poor population with 46.54% than the agricultural headed family with 45.31% of poor population.

The analysis of calorie gap ratio based on 2047 Kcal cutoff shows that agriculturalist have higher gap of 11.27% than the services with 8.23%. Thus, the depth of calorie deprivation for household headed by agriculturalist is 230.69 Kcal per poor person, while it is 168.47 Kcal per poor person for households headed by service. The estimation of calorie gap ratio based on 2044 Kcal cutoff shows a lower percentage for the household headed by agriculturalist and service. The figures in the table show that calorie gap is (229.75 Kcal) 11.24% and (167.81 Kcal) 8.21% per poor person for agricultural and service headed household respectively. However, the calorie gap ratio based on 2441.92 Kcal cutoff shows a higher ratio than the result based on National and

The calorie short fall is 12.96% per poor person for the households headed by service, while it is 15.50% in agricultural headed households. On comparison between service and agricultural headed calorie gap ratio based on different calorie norms, it is found that calorie gap ratio of the agricultural headed households is higher than the service headed households.

The estimation of Sen Index (P) based on 2047 Kcal cutoff shows that agricultural headed family have higher percentage of poor amongst the poor falling below their calorie norm with 8.78% than the service headed family with 7.01%. The estimation of Sen Index based on 2044 Kcal cutoff shows that 8.76% and 6.89% of the poor amongst the poor agricultural headed household and service headed household respectively are falling short of their calorie norms. However, the Sen Index based on 2441.92 Kcal cutoff reveals that the percentage of poor amongst the poor falling below their calorie norm in agricultural headed family is 12.09%, while it is 11.04% for the service headed family. The comparison between service and agricultural headed Sen Index based on different calorie norms reveal that percentage of poor amongst the poor is higher in agricultural headed households than the service headed households.

The analysis of P^F based on 2047 Kcal cutoff shows that severity of calorie deprivation is higher in agricultural headed family than the service headed family. It can be seen from the table that severity of calorie inadequacy falls on 6.96% of the poorest poor for the agricultural headed family, while it is 4.42% for the service headed family. The estimation of P^F based on 2044 Kcal cutoff shows that 6.94% and 4.41% of the poorest poor for the agricultural headed household and service headed household respectively are facing calorie inadequacy. However, the P^F based on 2441.92 Kcal cutoff shows a higher calorie deprivation than the result based on National and State calorie norms. The percentage of the poorest poor facing calorie inadequacy in agricultural headed family is 8.86%, while it is 8.88% for the service headed family. The comparison between service and agricultural headed household in the severity of calorie deprivation based on different calorie norms reveal that percentage of the poorest poor is higher in agricultural headed household than the service headed household when the calorie norm is 2044 Kcal and 2047. But in 2441.92 Kcal norms, percentage of the poorest poor is higher in service headed households than the agricultural headed households.

Thus, it is seen that the use of different calorie norms influence the magnitude of Head Count Ratio, Calorie Gap, Sen index and Foster, Greer and Thorbacke measures. It is clear from the above explanation that the extent, depth and severity of calorie deprivation is lower, when the estimation is based on State and National calorie norms. Whereas, the estimation based on sample survey norms show a higher deprivation among the selected category.

2. Measuring Poverty through MPCE

In measuring the poor among the sample population, the estimation of MPCE/poverty line by NSSO and the sample survey are used. The resultant figures of the analysis are given in the following Table 4.3.

(a) Sample population

The estimation of Head Count Ratio (HCR) based on the poverty line of Rs. 558.78 shows that 2.04% of the sample populations are poor. While HCR based on poverty line of Rs. 1010.81 shows that 67.18% of the sample populations are poor. However, the HCR based on the poverty line of Rs. 942.60 reveals that 59.54% of the sample populations are poor. This percentage of poor is higher than the percentage of poor estimated using the National poverty line by 57.50% but lower than the estimated percentage of poor based on State poverty line by 7.64%.

The analysis of poverty gap ratio based on National poverty line is .13% per poor person. This means that every poor person is falling short of the income by Rs. 0.73. In other words, to support every poor person at the poverty line, Rs. 0.72 of income is needed per poor person. The estimation of poverty Gap ratio based on State poverty line shows a higher income deprivation for the sample

Table 4.3
Measuring Poverty through MPCE

Category	*Head Count Ratio (HCR)*			*Poverty Gap (PG)*			*Sen Index (P)*			*Foster, Greer and Thorbecke (P^F)*		
	1	*2*	*3*	*1*	*2*	*3*	*1*	*2*	*3*	*1*	*2*	*3*
Sample population	.0204	.6718	.5954	.0013	.1382	.1009	.0011	.1189	.0868	.00013	.0522	.042
Gender-wise												
Male	.0116	.686	.6279	.00004	.1398	.1012	.00004	.1219	.0882	.000002	.0349	.0219
Female	.0271	.6606	.5701	.0019	.1369	.1006	.0016	.1181	.0868	.000023	.0366	.0242
Village-wise												
Longsa	.0309	.6216	.5792	.0019	.1421	.1078	.0058	.1209	.0919	.000206	.0393	.0263
Yunchuchu	0	.7381	.5714	0	.1313	.0874	0	.1195	.0796	0	.0283	.0159
Sunglup	0	.8947	.7632	0	.1339	.0846	0	.1222	.0775	0	.0268	.0144
Bhandari	0	.5741	.5741	0	.2112	.0883	0	.1048	.0765	0	.0311	.0199
Range-wise												
Upper	.0309	.6216	.5792	.0019	.1421	.1078	.0058	.1209	.0919	.000206	.0393	.0263
Middle	0	.8125	.6625	0	.1325	.0863	0	.1929	.1386	0	.0276	.0152
Lower	0	.5741	.5741	0	.2112	.0883	0	.1048	.0765	0	.0311	.0199

(Contd...)

	1	*2*	*3*	*1*	*2*	*3*	*1*	*2*	*3*	*1*	*2*	*3*
Sex-wise head of household												
Male headed family	.0192	.6613	.5879	.00079	.1355	.0985	.0028	.1172	.0854	.00003	.0349	.0225
Female headed family	.025	.7125	.625	.0031	.1487	.1092	.0051	.1289	.0947	.00054	.0552	.0258
Occupation-wise head of household												
Service	0	.7547	.4969	0	.08001	.0535	0	.0719	.0481	0	.0375	.0319
Agricultural	.0342	.735	.6752	.0021	.1616	.1206	.0019	.1454	.1085	.00021	.0439	.293

Source: Field survey 2005-06

1 – Poverty line of Rs 558.78 (National Poverty Line)

2 - Poverty line of Rs 1010.81(State Poverty Line)

3 - Poverty line of Rs 942.6 (Sample Survey Poverty Line)

population with 13.82% per poor person. However, the poverty gap ratio based on sample survey poverty line with 10.09% shows a lower income deprivation for the sample population than the estimation based on State poverty line but higher than the estimation based on National poverty line. It means to support every poor person at the poverty level, income of Rs. 95.11 per poor person is required.

From Table 4.3 it is seen that Sen Index (P) based on National poverty line for the sample population is 0.11%. This means that 0.11% of poor amongst the poor are falling below their poverty line. The P based on the State poverty line shows that the extent of income deprivation for the sample population is 21.22%. It means that 21.22% of poor amongst the poor are falling below their poverty line. However, the P based on sample survey poverty line shows that 16.94% of poor amongst the poor are living below their poverty line. Thus, P based on state poverty line shows a higher percentage of poor amongst the poor than the P based on National poverty line by 21.11% and sample survey poverty line by 4.28%.

The estimation of Foster, Greer and Thorbecke measure (P^F) based on National poverty line shows that the severity of income inadequacy for the sample population is 0.01% for the poorest poor. This means that 0 01% of the poorest poor are far below the poverty line. The P^F based on the State poverty line shows that the severity of income inadequacy for the sample population is 5.22% for the poorest poor. However, the P^F based on sample survey poverty line shows that income inadequacy with 4.2% is less severe than the estimation based on State poverty line but more severe than the estimation based on National poverty line.

(b) Gender-wise

The analysis of HCR based on the pôverty line of Rs. 558.78 shows that 1.16% of the male population is poor, while 2.71% of the female population is poor. The estimation ·f HCR based on poverty line of Rs. 1010.81 shows that that male (68.6%) have a higher percentage of poor than female (66.06%) by 2.54%. The estimation of HCR using Rs. 942.60 poverty line shows that 62.79%

of male population is poor whereas 57.01% of female population is poor. Comparison between male and female percentage of poor based on different poverty line reveals that the percentage of poor is higher among male than female when poverty line is based on Rs.1010.81 and Rs. 942.6. But the percentage of poor is higher among female than male when poverty line is based on Rs. 558.78.

The income gap ratio estimates based on National poverty line for male and female shows that female have higher ratio of .19% per person than male ratio of .004% per person. It means to help every poor person at the poverty level, income of Rs. 1.062 per poor person and Rs.0.022 per poor person respectively, is required by female and male poor population. However, poverty gap ratio based on State poverty line shows a higher percentage for both male and female population. The figures in the table show that poverty gap is (Rs. 141.31) 13.98% and (Rs. 138.38) 13.69% per poor person for male and female population respectively. Whereas, the poverty gap ratio based on sample survey poverty line shows a lower income shortfall for both male and female population with 10.12% and 10.06% per poor person respectively. It means to support every male poor person at the poverty level 10.12% of income is required while it is 10.06% per person for the female poor. On comparison between male and female poverty gap ratio based on State and sample survey poverty line, it is seen that the poverty gap ratio of male is higher than female.

The analysis of P based on National poverty line shows that female have higher percentage (.16%) of poor amongst the poor falling below their poverty line than male percentage (.004%). The estimation of P based on State poverty line shows a higher percentage for both male and female population. The figure in the table indicates that male have 12.19% of poor amongst the poor are falling short of their poverty line that is slightly higher than female percentage of 11.81%. However, P based sample survey poverty line shows that male population have 8.82% of poor amongst the poor falling below their poverty line, while female have 8.68% of poor amongst the poor falling below the poverty line. The comparison between male and female Sen Index based on State and sample survey poverty line shows that Sen Index of male is higher than female across different poverty lines.

The P^F estimates based on National poverty line shows that income deprivation is more severe for female population than male population. The analysis shows that the severity of income inadequacy falls on 0.0023 % of the poorest poor among the female population, while it is 0.0002% for the male population. The estimation of P^F based on State poverty line shows a similar result with large difference. The income inadequacy for both male and female comes out to be 3.49% and 3.66% for the poorest poor respectively. However, P^F based on sample poverty line shows that severity of income inadequacy falls on 2.19% of the poorest poor in male population, while it is 2.42% for the female population. The comparison between male and female P^F based on different poverty lines shows that the income inadequacy of female is higher than male.

(c) Village-wise

The HCR estimate based on National poverty line for the sample villages shows that only Longsa exhibits the existence of poor population with 3.09%, while other villages shows that every one is above the poverty line. The estimation of HCR based on State poverty lines for different villages shows that Sunglup with 89.47% has the highest proportion of population below poverty line. This is followed by Yunchuchu with 73.81% and Longsa with 62.16% of population below the poverty line. Bhandari shows the lowest proportion of poor with 57.41%. However, the estimation of HCR based on sample survey poverty line shows Sunglup with 76.32% has the highest percentage of poor among the villages. It is followed by Longsa with 57.92% and Bhandari with 57.41% of the population living below the poverty line. Yunchuchu with 57.14% shows the lowest percentage of poor people living below the poverty line. On comparing the proportion of poor among different villages based on poverty line of the State and Sample survey, it is seen from the table that Sunglup exhibits highest existence of poverty.

The poverty gap ratio estimates based on National poverty line shows that, the depth of income deprivation exist only in Longsa with (Rs. 1.06) .19% per poor person. The estimation of poverty gap using State poverty line shows that the depth of income deprivation is highest in Bhandari with (Rs. 213.28) 21.12% per person. It is followed by Longsa with (Rs. 143.64) 14.21% per poor person and Sunglup with (Rs. 135.35) 13.39% per poor person. Yunchuchu with (Rs. 132.72) 13.13% per poor person exhibits the lowest income deprivation among the villages. However, the estimation of poverty gap ratio based on sample survey poverty indicates a higher income deprivation among the sample population than the estimation based on National poverty line but lower than the estimation based on State poverty line. Among the villages, Longsa with (Rs. 101.61) 10.78% per poor person shows the highest shortfall of income. This is followed by Bhandari with (Rs. 83.23) 8.83% per poor person and Yunchuchu with (Rs. 82.38) 8.74% per poor person. Sunglup with (Rs. 79.74) 8.46% shows the lowest income deprivation among the villages. On comparison among the villages it is seen that the highest depth of income deprivation exist in Bhandari when measurement is based on State poverty line. However, the estimation of poverty gap ratio based on sample survey poverty and National poverty line indicates that Longsa has the highest shortfall of income.

The estimation of Sen Index (P) based on National poverty line shows that, the extent of income deprivation exist only in Longsa with 0.58% of poor amongst the poor falling below their poverty line. The P based on State poverty line shows that, among the villages, Sunglup with 12.22% exhibits the highest percentage of poor amongst the poor falling below their poverty line. It is followed by Longsa with 12.09% and Yunchuchu with 11.95% of poor amongst the poor falling below their poverty line. Bhandari with 10.48% of poor amongst the poor falling below their poverty line exhibits the lowest percentage among the villages. However, the estimation of P based on sample survey poverty line indicates a higher percentage of poor amongst the poor than the estimation based on National poverty line but lower than the estimation based on State poverty line. Among the villages, Longsa with 9.19% have the highest percentage of poor amongst the poor falling below their poverty line. This is followed by Yunchuchu with 7.96% and Sunglup with 7.75% of poor amongst the poor falling below their poverty line. Bhandari with 7.65% of poor amongst the poor falling below their poverty line shows the lowest percentage among the villages. On comparing among the villages, it was found that Sunglup has the highest number of poor amongst the poor when measurement is based on State poverty line, while Longsa exhibit the highest number of poor amongst the poor when measured at the sample survey poverty line.

Village-wise analysis of P^F based on National poverty line shows that, the severity of income deprivation exist only in Longsa with 0.02% of the poorest poor. The P^F based on State poverty line shows that, among the villages, income inadequacy is more severe in Longsa with 3.93% of the poorest poor. It means 3.93% of the poorest poor in Longsa are far below the poverty line. It is followed by Bhandari with 3.11% and Yunchuchu with 2.83% of the poorest poor facing income inadequacy. Sunglup with 2.68% of the poorest poor facing income inadequacy exhibits the lowest severity of income deprivation among the villages. However, the estimation of P^F based on sample survey poverty line indicates a higher severity of income deprivation than the estimation based on National poverty line but lower than the estimation based on State poverty line. Among the villages, Income inadequacy is more severe in Longsa with 2.63% of the poorest poor. It means 2.63% of the poorest Longsa are far below the poverty line. It is followed by Bhandari with 1.99% and Yunchuchu with 1.59% of the poorest poor facing income inadequacy. Sunglup with 1.44% of the poorest poor facing income inadequacy exhibits the lowest severity of income deprivation among the villages. On comparison among the villages it was found that Longsa exhibits higher severity of income deprivation, while Sunglup has a lower income inadequacy across different poverty lines.

(d) Range-wise

Range-wise estimation of poverty is shown in the Table 4.3.

From the table it is clear that the upper range is represented by Longsa village and lower range is represented by Bhandari village. Thus, the explanation given for these villages also represents their respective range. However, middle range is represented by two villages, viz, Yunchuchu and Sunglup.

The HCR estimate based on National poverty line for the sample villages shows that only upper range exhibits the existence of poor population with 3.09%, while other ranges shows that every one is above the poverty line. The estimation of HCR based on State poverty lines shows that middle range with 81.25% has the highest proportion of population below poverty line. This is followed by upper range with 62.16% and lower range with 57.41% of population below the poverty line. Moreover, the estimation of HCR based on sample survey poverty line also shows that middle range with 66.25% has the highest percentage of poor among the ranges. It is followed by upper range with 57.92% and lower range with 57.41% of the population living below the poverty line. On comparing the proportion of poor among different ranges based on poverty line of the State and Sample survey, it is seen from the table that middle range exhibits highest existence of poverty.

The poverty gap ratio estimates based on National poverty line shows that, the depth of income deprivation exist only in upper range with (Rs. 1.06) .19% per poor person. The estimation of poverty gap using State poverty line shows that the depth of income deprivation is highest in lower range with (Rs. 213.28) 21.12% per person. It is followed by upper range with (Rs. 143.64) 14.21% per poor person. Middle range with (Rs. 133.93) 13.25% per poor person exhibits the lowest income deprivation among the ranges. However, the estimation of poverty gap ratio based on sample survey poverty indicates a higher income deprivation among the sample ranges than the estimation based on National poverty line but lower than the estimation based on State poverty line. Among the ranges, upper range with (Rs. 101.61) 10.78% per poor person shows the highest shortfall of income. This is followed by lower range with (Rs. 83.23) 8.83% per poor person. Lower range with (Rs. 81.35) 8.63% shows the lowest income deprivation among the ranges.

On comparison among the ranges it is seen that the highest depth of income deprivation exist in lower range when measurement is based on State poverty line. However, the estimation of poverty gap ratio based on sample survey poverty line and National poverty line indicates that upper range has the highest shortfall of income per person.

The estimation of Sen Index (P) based on National poverty line shows that, the extent of income deprivation exist only in upper range with 0.58% of poor amongst the poor falling below their poverty line. The P based on State poverty line shows that, middle range with 19.29% exhibits the highest percentage of poor amongst the poor falling below their poverty line. It is followed by upper range with 12.09% of poor amongst the poor falling below their poverty line. Lower range with 10.48% of poor amongst the poor falling below their poverty line exhibits the lowest percentage among the ranges. However, the estimation of P based on sample survey poverty line indicates a higher percentage of poor amongst the poor than the estimation based on National poverty line but lower than the estimation based on State poverty line. Among the ranges, middle range with 13.86% has the highest percentage of poor amongst the poor falling below their poverty line. This is followed by upper range with 9.19% of poor amongst the poor falling below their poverty line. Lower range with 7.65% of poor amongst the poor falling below their poverty line shows the lowest percentage among the ranges. On comparing among the ranges, it was found that middle range has the highest number of poor amongst the poor when measurement is based on State poverty line and sample survey poverty line.

Range-wise analysis of P^F based on National poverty line shows that, the severity of income deprivation exist only in upper range with 0.02% of the poorest poor. The P^F based on State poverty line shows that, among the ranges, income inadequacy is more severe in upper range with 3.93% of the poorest poor. It is followed by lower range with 3.11% of the poorest poor facing income inadequacy. Middle range with 2.76% of the poorest poor facing income inadequacy exhibits the lowest severity of income deprivation among the ranges. However, the estimation of P^F based on sample survey poverty line indicates a higher severity of income deprivation than the estimation based on National poverty line but lower than the estimation based on State poverty line. Among the ranges, Income inadequacy is more severe in upper range with 2.63% of the poorest poor. It is followed by lower range with 1.99% of the poorest poor facing income inadequacy. Middle range with 1.52% of the poorest poor facing income inadequacy exhibits the lowest severity of income deprivation among the ranges. On comparison among the ranges it was found that upper range exhibits higher severity of income deprivation, while lower range has a lower income inadequacy across different poverty lines.

(e) Sex-wise Head of Household

Estimation of HCR based on National, State and sample survey poverty lines shows that the proportion of poor is higher in female headed family than male headed family. Using the National poverty line, Table 4.3 shows that 2.5% of the populations in female headed family are living below the poverty line, while male headed family has 1.92% of poor people. The estimation of HCR using State poverty line shows that 71.25% population in female headed family are living below the poverty line, while it is 66.13% for the male headed family. However, the estimation of HCR based on Sample survey poverty line shows a lower percentage of poor living below the poverty line than the estimation based on State poverty line. The percentage of poor based on sample survey poverty line is 62.5% for female headed family and 58.79% for male headed family. Thus, the existence of higher poor is seen among the female headed household.

The sex-wise head of household estimation of poverty gap ratio based on the National poverty line shows that the depth of income deprivation higher in female headed family than male headed family. Table 4.3 shows that the depth of income deprivation in female headed family is 0.31% (Rs. 1.73) per poor person, while it is 0.08% (Rs. 0.44) per poor person for male headed family. The estimation of poverty gap ratio using State poverty line shows that the income shortfall of the population in female headed family is (Rs. 150.31) 14.87% per poor person, while it is (Rs. 136.96) 13.55% per poor person in male headed family. The estimation of poverty gap ratio based on Sample survey poverty line shows a lower gap than the estimation based on State poverty line. The female headed household has an income shortfall of (Rs. 102.93) 10.92% per poor person, while it is (Rs. 92.85) 9.85% per poor person. Thus, it can be seen that female headed households have higher income deprivation as compared to male headed households across different poverty lines.

The estimation of P based on the National poverty line reveals that the percentage of poor amongst the poor falling below their poverty line is higher in female headed family than male headed family. It can be seen from Table 4.3 that the percentage of poor amongst the poor falling below their poverty line in female headed family is .051%, while it is .028% for the male headed family. The estimation of P using State poverty line shows that the number of poor amongst the poor falling below their poverty line in female headed family is 12.89%, while it is 11.72% for the male headed family. The estimation of P based on Sample survey poverty line shows a lower P than the estimation based on State poverty line. The female headed household has 9.47% of poor amongst the poor living below their poverty line, while 8.54% of the poor amongst the poor in male headed family are below their poverty line. Thus, the estimation of Sen Index based on different poverty line shows that female headed households has higher percentage of poor amongst the poor than male headed households.

The estimation of P^F on the National poverty line shows that the severity of income deprivation higher in female headed family than male headed family. It can be seen from table No. 4.2.2 that the severity of income deprivation in female headed family is 0.05% of the poorest poor, while it is 0.003% for the male headed family. The estimation of P^F using State poverty line shows that the income inadequacy for the poorest poor in female headed family is 5.52%, while it is 3.49% for the male headed family. The estimation of P^F based on Sample survey poverty line shows a lower P^F than the estimation based on State poverty line. The female headed household has an income inadequacy of 2.58% of the poorest poor, while it is 2.25% for the male headed family. Thus measuring P^F basing on different poverty line shows that severity of income inadequacy is higher in female headed household than male headed household.

(f) Occupation-wise head of household

Estimation of HCR based on National poverty line shows that poverty exist only the household headed by agriculturalist with 3.42%. But the analysis of HCR based on State poverty line shows that the proportion of poor is higher in the household headed by services than the agriculturalist. From the table it is seen that the household headed by service have 75.47% of its population below the poverty line, whereas, those household headed by agriculturalist have 73.5% of its population living below the poverty line. However, the estimation of HCR based on the sample survey poverty line indicates that the proportion of poor is higher in the household headed by agriculturalist than the services. Table 4.3 shows the household headed agriculture has 65.52% of poor population, while it is 49.69% in service headed family. Thus, the estimation based on different poverty line gives a mix result.

The analysis of poverty gap ratio based on National poverty line shows that Income deprivation exists only in the household headed by the agriculturalist with .21% per person. From the table it is seen that the depth of income deprivation for household headed by agriculturalist is Rs. 1.24 per poor person. The estimation of poverty gap ratio based on State poverty line shows that income gap is 16.16% per poor person for agricultural headed family. For the household headed by service, the income shortfall of poverty line is 8% per poor person. However, the poverty gap ratio based on sample survey poverty line shows that the income shortfall of the households headed by service is 5.35% per poor person, where as it is 12.06% per poor person for agricultural headed household. On comparison between service and agricultural headed poverty gap ratio based on different poverty norms, it found that poverty gap ratio of the agricultural headed households is higher than the service headed households.

The estimation of P based on National poverty line shows that .19% of the poor amongst the poor in the households headed by the agriculturalist are below their poverty line. The estimation of Sen Index based on State poverty line shows that 14.54% and 7.19% of the poor amongst the poor in agricultural headed household and service headed household respectively are falling below their poverty line. Whereas, the Sen Index based on sample survey poverty line shows that the percentage of poor amongst the poor falling below their poverty line in agricultural headed family is 10.85%, while it is 4.71% for the service headed family. The comparison between service and agricultural headed household Sen Index based on different poverty line reveals that percentage of poor amongst the poor is higher in agricultural headed household than the service headed household.

The analysis of P^F based on National poverty line shows that severity of income deprivation falls on .02% of the poorest poor among the agricultural headed family; while the service headed family have zero poor population. The estimation of P^F based on State poverty line shows that 4.39% and 3.75% of the poorest among the poor in agricultural headed households and service headed households respectively are facing income inadequacy. However, the P^F based on sample survey poverty line shows a lower income deprivation than the result based on State poverty line. The percentage of the poorest poor facing income inadequacy in agricultural headed family is 2.93%, while it is 3.19% for the service headed family. The comparison between service and agricultural headed households in the severity of income deprivation based on different poverty line reveals that percentage of the poorest among the poor is higher in agricultural headed households than the service headed households when estimate is based on the State and National poverty line. But the percentage result based on the sample survey poverty line shows that the percentage of the poorest poor facing income deficiency is higher in service headed households than the agricultural headed households.

Thus, measuring poverty based on different poverty line shows that the extent and depth of poverty is higher when measurement is based on State poverty line. However, the extent and depth of poverty reveals a negligible existence of poor people when the estimation is based on National poverty line. Thus, the poverty line derived from the sample survey lies in between the National and State poverty lines.

Impact of Poverty Alleviation Programme

The provision of employment on public works has been advocated as a means of relieving poverty and famines in South Asia for at least a century.[2] Thus raising the standard of living of the masses is one of the main objectives of planning in India. The first scheme to directly reduce poverty was the Employment Guarantee Scheme introduced in 1972-73 by the Government of Maharashtra. It was the first of its kind to give recognition to the 'right to work' enshrine in the constitution.[3] Since then, the Government of India has been initiating many pro-poor programmes to reduce poverty in the Country; namely, National Rural Employment Programme (NREP) 1980, Integrated Rural Development Programme (IRDP) 1980, Rural Landless Employment Guarantee Programme (RLEP) 1983, Jawahar Rozgar Yojana (JRY) 1989, Swarn Jayanti Shahari Rozgar Yojana (1997), etc. The most recent programme announced to alleviate poverty in India came with the legislation of National Rural Employment Guarantee Act (NREGA) 2005. Since many programmes have been launched in the country to alleviate poverty, it becomes pertinent to examine the benefit from any of these programmes by the sample population. The analysis of the impact of poverty alleviation on the sample population has been shown in Table 4.4.

Table 4.4
Poverty alleviation Programme

Category	*Total Sample household*		*Longsa*		*Yunchuchu*		*Sunglup*		*Bhandari*	
	No	*%*	*No*	*%*	*No*	*%*	*No*	*%*	*No*	*%*
Households that has so far received Poverty Alleviation Programme	10	10.10	9	13.24	0	0	1	8.3	0	0
No of persons	16	4.07	15	5.79	0	0	1	2.63	0	0
Households that did not received Poverty Alleviation Programme	89	89.90	59	86.76	9	100	11	91.7	10	100
No of persons	377	95.93	244	94.21	42	100	37	97.37	54	100

Source: Field Survey 2005-06.
0: Nil

From the survey it was found that programme such as JRY and Below Poverty Line (Rice) have been implemented so far. Out of the total 99 households surveyed, only 10 households have been benefited from the implementation of poverty alleviation programme. This means that 89.90% of the households have not been benefited. The figures in the table reveals that only 4.07% of the total sample population have been benefited from the implementation of poverty alleviation programmes. Out of this 1.78% of the population got the help from JRY, while 2.29% of the population got the Below Poverty Line (Rice). Among the villages, Longsa with 9 households had received aids from the government accounting for 13.23% of its total households surveyed, tops in the performance of poverty alleviation programme. Thus, in Longsa 5.79% population were benefited from the implementation of poverty alleviation programmes. Out of this, 2.32% benefited from JRY, while 3.47% benefited from the Below Poverty Line (Rice). Sunglup followed next with 8.33% of its total households surveyed getting the benefits from JRY. But the percentage of population being benefited is low with only 2.63%. For the remaining two villages, surveyed showed a zero benefit from any such programmes by the sample population. It was also observed that out the total beneficiaries, 2.54% of the populations are below the poverty line. The resultant figure clearly reveals that only a meagre proportion of poor have been benefited from such programmes, while 64.64% (based on State Poverty line) of the poor or 57.73% (based on Sample survey poverty line) of the poor remained outside the parameter of the poverty alleviation programme. This clearly shows the failure of the poverty alleviation programme in giving the complete coverage to the poor people. One of the reasons is the leakage of benefits to non- poor, which is termed as the total dead weight loss.[4]

In conclusion, it can be said that estimation of poverty becomes vital in formulating suitable policy for eradicating poverty. The resultant proportion of poor, the shortfall of income and the severity of income deprivation throw light on the living standard of the people. This in turn helps in knowing not only the number of poor people but also their deprivation, which can be used by the government in formulation as well as implementation of any poverty alleviation programme.

NOTES

1. Dubey, A., Gangopadhyay, S. and Wadhwa, W. (2001); "Occupational Structure and Incidence of Poverty in Indian Towns of Different Sizes", *Review of Development Economics*, 5(1), p 49-59.

2. Bhatia, B.M. (1967). *Famines in India: A Study of Some Aspects of the Economic History of India (1860-1965)*, London: Asia publishing House. p. 120.
3. Bagchee, A. (2005); "Political and Administration Realities of Employment Guarantee Scheme", *Economic and Political Weekly*, Oct 15 issue 2005. Online [available] at www.epw.org.
4. Ravallion, M. (2002), "On the Coverage of Public Employment Schemes for Poverty Alleviation", in Subramanian S. (ed), *Measurement of Inequality and Poverty*, Oxford University Press, p.281.

5

Disparity in the Distribution of Calorie Intake and MPCE

Nature has created difference among people, among regions and among situations. The conditions of these natural differences are also called as constraints. However, man has always made efforts to minimise these constraints to advance on the path of development. On the other hand the differences created by man on account of social, economic, political, religious and cultural aspects are called not as differences but inequalities or disparities. These disparities are called respectively as social, economic, political, religious and cultural disparities. An economic disparity can be defined as a condition in which a person or persons though legally having equal rights is or are but for economic reasons deprived to some extent from available opportunities of fulfilling economic, social, political, cultural and religious needs. There are different types of economic disparity, viz, income and wealth disparity, education disparity, technological disparity, regional disparity and sectoral disparity. The main causes of this disparity are political, administrative, unequal distribution of natural resources and caste system. In this chapter, the extent to which the calorie intake and MPCE, most commonly measured by households or individual, is distributed in an uneven manner has been discussed thoroughly. Moreover, the relationship between the disparity in the distribution of calorie intake and MPCE with that of the proportion of poor has been estimated.

Measuring Inequality Through Calorie Intake

Inequalities in the distribution of calorie intake are being measured for different selected category.

(i) Distribution of Calorie Intake among the Sample Population: The cumulated percentages among the sample population as well as the daily calorie intake are presented in Table No. 5.1. The cumulated percentages calorie intake and population, when plotted on a graph paper gives the resultant shape which is evident from figure 18. This figure reveals that the bottom 14% of the population consumes about 4% of the total calorie intake at one end and at the other end about 17% of the total calorie intake is shared by the top 10%. Thus 90% of the population share 83% of the total calorie intake.

Table 5.1
Distribution of calorie intake among the Sample population

Calorie group	*Total number of person (F)*	*Total calorie intake (Q)*	*% of F*	*% of Q*	*Cf of F*	*Cf of Q*
0 – 500	15	3117.4	3.82	0.33	3.82	0.33
501 - 1000	16	11934.96	4.08	1.24	7.9	1.57
1001 – 1500	22	27767.46	5.59	2.89	13.49	4.46
1501 – 2000	56	99691.1	14.25	10.39	27.74	14.85
2001 – 2500	92	209987.1	23.41	21.88	51.15	36.73
2501 – 3000	87	239188.7	22.14	24.92	73.29	61.65
3001 – 3500	63	204667.8	16.03	21.32	89.32	82.97
3501 – 4000	31	113319.1	7.89	11.82	97.21	94.79
4000 and above	11	50000.66	2.79	5.21	100	100

Sources: Field Survey 2005-06.

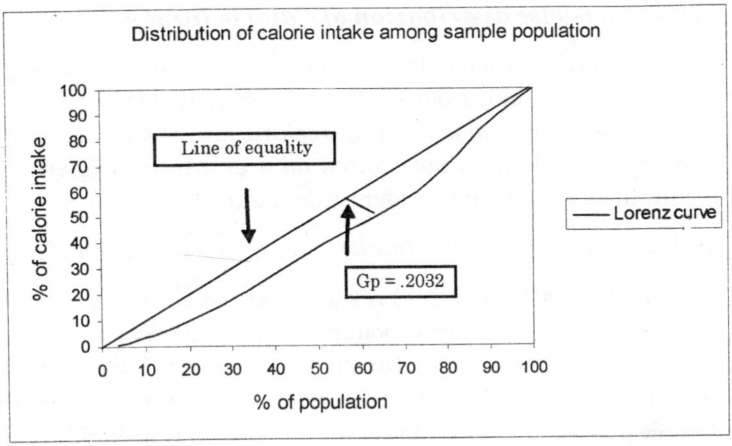

Figure 18: Distribution of calorie intake among the Sample population.

The value of Gini-coefficient (Gp) for calorie intake among the sample population has been worked with the help of the following formulas:

$$\text{Gini Coefficient (Gp)} = \frac{\text{Area between Lorenz Curve and Diagonal}}{\text{Total Area under Diagonal}}$$

Area between Lorenz Curve and Diagonal (G) is given by;

$$G = \sum_{i=1}^{n-1} (F_i Q_{i+1} - F_{i+1} Q_i)$$

$$Gp = \frac{28861.36 - 26650.12}{100 \text{ X } 100}$$

$$Gp = .2032.$$

The value of Gini-coefficient (Gp) for calorie intake among the sample population has been worked out as .2032. Both Gini-coefficients and the shape of Lorenz curve show high inequality in the distribution of calorie intake among the sample population.

(ii) Gender-wise distribution of Calorie Intake

The cumulated percentages among the population of male and female and their daily calorie intake are presented in Table 5.2 (a and b). The cumulated percentages calorie intake and population of male and female, when plotted on a graph paper gives the resultant shape which is evident from figure 19.

(a) Distribution of Calorie Intake among the Population of Male

The data in Table 5.2 (a) reveals that the bottom 15% of the male population consumes about 5% of the total calorie intake at one end. But at the other end about 14% of the total calorie intake is shared by the top 8%, which is lower than the percentage of the sample population. Thus 92% of the population shares 86% of the total calorie intake, which is higher than the sample population share.

The value of Gini-coefficient (Gp) for calorie intake among male population has been worked with the help of the following formulas:

$$\text{Gini Coefficient (Gp)} = \frac{\text{Area between Lorenz Curve and Diagonal}}{\text{Total Area under Diagonal}}$$

$$Gp = \frac{29395.16 - 27328.16}{100 \text{ X } 100}$$

$$Gp = .2067.$$

The value of Gini-coefficient (Gp) for calorie intake among the sample population has been worked out as .2067. Both Gini-coefficients and the shape of Lorenz curve show higher inequality in the distribution of calorie intake among the male population than the sample population. The figure 19 represents the Lorenz curve of male.

Table 5.2 (a)
Distribution of Calorie Intake among the Population of Male

Calorie group	*Total number of person (F)*	*Total calorie intake (Q)*	*% of F*	*% of Q*	*Cf of F*	*Cf of Q*
0 – 500	5	1610.19	2.91	0.38	2.91	0.38
501 – 1000	10	7242.53	5.81	1.74	8.72	2.12
1001 – 1500	11	13810.99	6.39	3.3	15.11	5.42
1501 – 2000	24	44183.7	13.95	10.59	29.07	16.01
2001 – 2500	42	95025.71	24.42	22.76	53.49	38.77
2501 – 3000	32	87664.09	18.60	20.99	72.09	59.76
3001 – 3500	33	107873.7	19.19	25.84	91.28	85.6
3501 – 4000	12	44151.49	6.98	10.58	98.26	96.18
4000 and above	3	15964.99	1.74	3.82	100	100

Sources: Field Survey 2005-06.

Table 5.2 (b)
Distribution of Calorie Intake among the Population of Female

Calorie group	*Total number of person (F)*	*Total calorie intake (Q)*	*% of F*	*% of Q*	*Cf of F*	*Cf of Q*
0 – 500	10	1507.21	4.52	0.28	4.52	0.28
501 - 1000	6	4692.43	2.71	0.86	7.23	1.14
1001 – 1500	11	13956.47	4.98	2.57	12.22	3.71
1501 – 2000	33	58098.67	14.93	10.70	27.15	14.41
2001 – 2500	50	114961.4	22.62	21.17	49.77	35.58
2501 – 3000	54	149834.3	24.44	27.59	74.21	63.17
3001 – 3500	30	96794.1	13.57	17.82	87.78	80.99
3501 – 4000	19	69167.57	8.61	12.74	96.38	93.73
4000 and above	8	34035.67	3.62	6.27	100	100

Sources: Field Survey 2005-06.

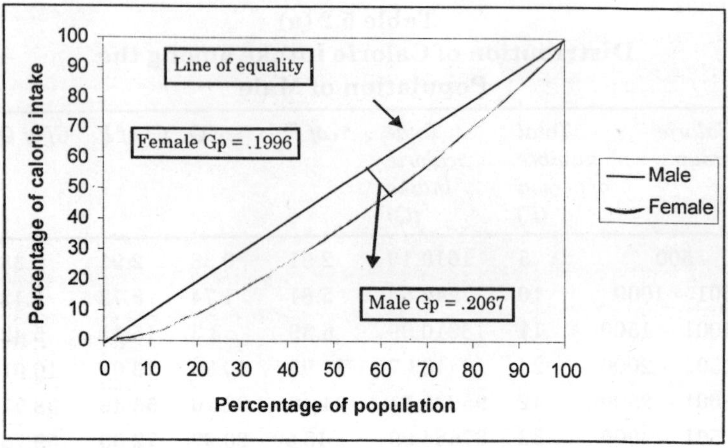

Figure 19: Gender-wise distribution of calorie intake.

(b) Distribution of Calorie Intake among the Population of Female

The data in Table 5.2 (b) reveals that the bottom 12% of the female population consumes about 3% of the total calorie intake at one end. But at the other end about 19% of the total calorie intake is shared by the top 10%, which is higher than the percentage of the sample population. Thus 90% of the population shares 81% of the total calorie intake, which is lower than the sample population share.

The value of Gini-coefficient (Gp) for calorie intake among female population has been worked as follows:

$$\text{Gini Coefficient (Gp)} = \frac{\text{Area between Lorenz Curve and Diagonal}}{\text{Total Area under Diagonal}}$$

$$Gp = \frac{28193.92 - 26198.14}{100 \text{ X } 100}$$

$$Gp = .1996.$$

The value of Gini-coefficient of calorie intake for the population of female comes out to be .1996. Both Gini-coefficients and the shape of Lorenz curve show lower inequality in the distribution of calorie intake among the female population than the sample and male population. The yellow line in figure 19 represents the Lorenz curve of female.

(iii) Village-wise distribution of Calorie Intake

The cumulated percentages among the population of Longsa, Yunchuchu, Sunglup and Bhandari villages and their daily calorie intake are presented in Table No. 5.3 (a, b, c and d). The cumulated percentages calorie intake and population of these villages, when plotted on a graph paper gives the resultant shape, which is evident from figure 20.

(a) Distribution of calorie intake among the population of Longsa village

The data in Table no 5.3 (a) reveals that the bottom 14% of the population consumes about 4% of the total calorie intake at one end that is similar to the percentage of the sample population. But at the other end about 16% of the total calorie intake is shared by the top 10%, which is slightly lower than the percentage of the sample population. Thus 90% of the population share 84% of the total calorie intake.

The value of Gini-coefficient (Gp) for calorie intake among the population of Longsa village has been worked as follows:

$$\text{Gini Coefficient (Gp)} = \frac{\text{Area between Lorenz Curve and Diagonal}}{\text{Total Area under Diagonal}}$$

$$Gp = \frac{28372.88 - 26256.39}{100 \text{ X } 100}$$

$$Gp = .2116.$$

The value of Gini-coefficient of calorie intake for the population of Longsa village comes out to be .2116. Both Gini-coefficients and the shape of Lorenz curve show higher inequality in the distribution of calorie intake among the population of Longsa village than the sample, male and female population. The red line in figure 20 represents the Lorenz curve of Longsa village.

Table 5.3 (a)
Distribution of Calorie Intake among the Population of Longsa village

Calorie group	*Total number of person (F)*	*Total calorie intake (Q)*	*% of F*	*% of Q*	*Cf of F*	*Cf of Q*
0 – 500	15	4199.33	5.8	0.67	5.8	0.67
501 - 1000	7	4948.66	2.71	0.79	8.51	1.46
1001 – 1500	14	17385.51	5.41	2.76	13.92	4.22
1501 – 2000	36	63267.69	13.89	10.06	27.81	14.28
2001 – 2500	64	145821.75	24.71	23.18	52.52	37.46
2501 – 3000	46	126591.71	17.76	20.13	70.28	57.59
3001 – 3500	51	164756.93	19.69	26.19	89.97	83.78
3501 – 4000	18	66037.48	6.95	10.51	96.92	94.29
4000 and above	8	35998.24	3.08	5.71	100	100

Sources: Field Survey 2005-06.

Table 5.3 (b)
Distribution of calorie intake among the population of Yunchuchu village

Calorie group	*Total number of person (F)*	*Total calorie intake (Q)*	*% of F*	*% of Q*	*Cf of F*	*Cf of Q*
0 – 500	1	0	2.38	0	2.38	0
501 - 1000	4	3217.07	9.53	3.3	11.91	3.3
1001 – 1500	5	6328.23	11.9	6.49	23.81	9.79
1501 – 2000	2	3512.48	4.76	3.6	28.57	13.39
2001 – 2500	13	30154.73	30.96	30.96	59.53	44.35
2501 – 3000	7	18867.05	16.67	19.37	76.2	63.72
3001 – 3500	4	13470.48	9.53	13.84	85.73	77.56
3501 and above	6	21846.47	14.27	22.44	100	100

Sources: Field Survey 2005-06.

Table 5.3 (c)
Distribution of calorie intake among the population of Sunglup village

Calorie group	*Total number of person (F)*	*Total calorie intake (Q)*	*% of F*	*% of Q*	*Cf of F*	*Cf of Q*
0 – 500	0	0	0	0	0	0
501 - 1000	2	1861.22	5.26	1.77	5.26	1.77
1001 – 1500	0	0	0	0	5.26	1.77
1501 – 2000	6	10957.84	15.79	10.42	21.05	12.19
2001 – 2500	3	12819.06	7.89	12.19	28.94	24.38
2501 – 3000	16	42544.87	42.12	40.45	71.06	64.83
3001 – 3500	9	29193.01	23.68	27.76	94.74	92.59
3501 – 4000	1	3700.57	2.63	3.52	97.37	96.11
4000 and above	1	4089.5	2.63	3.89	100	100

Sources: Field Survey 2005-06.

Table 5.3 (d)
Distribution of calorie intake among the population of Bhandari village

Calorie group	*Total number of person (F)*	*Total calorie intake (Q)*	*% of F*	*% of Q*	*Cf of F*	*Cf of Q*
0 – 500	1	0	1.9	0	1.9	0
501 - 1000	1	826.08	1.9	0.62	3.8	0.62
1001 – 1500	3	4053.72	5.6	3.02	9.4	3.64
1501 – 2000	12	21953.09	22.2	16.38	31.6	20.02
2001 – 2500	12	27038.97	22.2	20.19	53.8	40.21
2501 – 3000	17	48432.51	31.4	36.16	85.2	76.37
3001 – 3500	0	0	0	0	85.2	76.37
3501 – 4000	6	21734.54	11.1	16.23	96.3	92.6
4000 and above	2	9912.92	3.7	7.4	100	100

Sources: Field Survey 2005-06.

(b) Distribution of calorie intake among the population of Yunchuchu village

The data in Table 5.3 (b) reveals that the bottom 12% of the population consumes about 3% of the total calorie intake at one end that is lower than the percentage of the sample population. But at the other end about 22% of the total calorie intake is shared by the top 14%, which is higher than the percentage of the sample population. Thus 86% of the population share 78% of the total calorie intake.

The value of Gini-coefficient (Gp) for calorie intake among the population of Yunchuchu village has been worked as follows:

$$\text{Gini Coefficient (Gp)} = \frac{\text{Area between Lorenz Curve and Diagonal}}{\text{Total Area under Diagonal}}$$

$$Gp = \frac{19986.67 - 17753.57}{100 \text{ X } 100}$$

$$Gp = .2233.$$

The value of the Gini-coefficient of calorie intake for the population of Yunchuchu village comes out to be .2233. Both Gini-coefficients and the shape of Lorenz curve show higher inequality in the distribution of calorie intake among the population of Yunchuchu village than the sample, male, female and Longsa population. The figure 20 represents the Lorenz curve of Yunchuchu village.

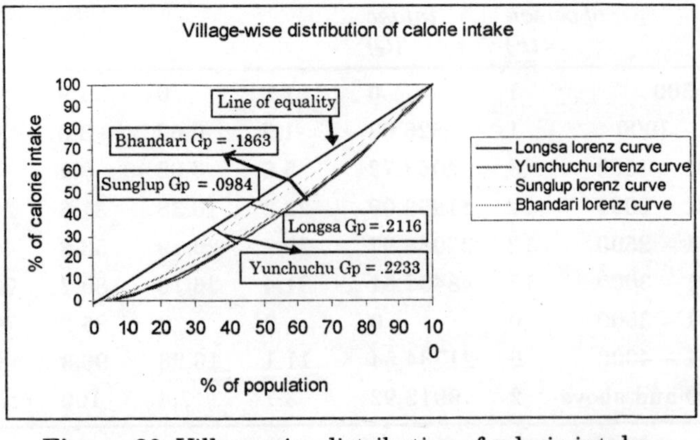

Figure 20: Village-wise distribution of calorie intake.

(c) Distribution of calorie intake among the population of Sunglup village

The data in Table 5.3 (c) reveals that the bottom 21% of the population consumes about 12% of the total calorie intake at one end that is higher than the percentage of the sample population. But at the other end about 7% of the total calorie intake is shared by the top 5%, which is lower than the percentage of the sample population. Thus 95% of the population share 93% of the total calorie intake.

The value of Gini-coefficient (Gp) for calorie intake among the population of Sunglup village has been worked as follows:

$$\text{Gini Coefficient (Gp)} = \frac{\text{Area between Lorenz Curve and Diagonal}}{\text{Total Area under Diagonal}}$$

$$Gp = \frac{27884.72 - 26900.27}{100 \text{ X } 100}$$

$$Gp = .0984.$$

The value of Gini-coefficient of calorie intake for the population of Sunglup village comes out to be .0984. Both Gini-coefficients and the shape of Lorenz curve shows lower inequality in the distribution of calorie intake among the population of Sunglup village than the sample, male, female, Longsa and Yunchuchu population. The yellow line in figure 20 represents the Lorenz curve of Sunglup village.

(d) Distribution of calorie intake among the population of Bhandari village

The data in Table 5.3 (d) reveals that the bottom 9% of the population consumes about 3% of the total calorie intake at one end that is higher than the percentage of the sample population. But at the other end about 7% of the total calorie intake is shared by the top 3%, which is higher than the percentage of the sample population. Thus 96% of the populations share 92% of the total calorie intake.

The value of Gini-coefficient (Gp) for calorie intake among the population of Bhandari village has been worked following the formulas:

$$\text{Gini Coefficient (Gp)} = \frac{\text{Area between Lorenz Curve and Diagonal}}{\text{Total Area under Diagonal}}$$

$$Gp = \frac{29608.78 - 27744.98}{100 \text{ X } 100}$$

$$Gp = .1863.$$

The value of Gini-coefficient of calorie intake for the population of Bhandari village has been worked out at .1863. Both Gini-coefficients and the shape of Lorenz curve shows higher inequality in the distribution of calorie intake among the population of Bhandari village than Sunglup village but lower inequalities than the sample, male, female, Longsa and Yunchuchu population. The rose line in figure 20 represents the Lorenz curve of Bhandari village.

(iv) Range-wise distribution of calorie intake

Range-wise estimation of inequalities in the distribution of calorie intake is shown in the Table no 5.4 (a, b and c). The cumulated percentages calorie intake and population of these ranges, when plotted on a graph paper gives the resultant shape which is evident from figure 21.

(a) Distribution of calorie intake among the population of upper range

The data in Table 5.4 (a) reveals that the bottom 14% of the population consumes about 4% of the total calorie intake at one end that is similar to the percentage of the sample population. But at the other end about 16% of the total calorie intake is shared by the top 10%, which is slightly lower than the percentage of the sample population. Thus 90% of the population share 84% of the total calorie intake.

The value of Gini-coefficient (Gp) for calorie intake among the population of upper range has been worked as follows:

$$\text{Gini Coefficient (Gp)} = \frac{\text{Area between Lorenz Curve and Diagonal(G)}}{\text{Total Area under Diagonal}}$$

$$Gp = \frac{28372.88 - 26256.39}{100 \text{ X } 100}$$

$$Gp = .2116.$$

The value of Gini-coefficient of calorie intake for the population of upper range comes out to be .2116. Both Gini-coefficients and the shape of Lorenz curve show higher inequality in the distribution of calorie intake among the population of upper range than the sample, male and female population. The red line in figure 21 represents the Lorenz curve of upper range.

Table 5.4 (a)
Distribution of calorie intake among the population of Upper range

Calorie group	*Total number of person (F)*	*Total calorie intake (Q)*	*% of F*	*% of Q*	*Cf of F*	*Cf of Q*
0 – 500	15	4199.33	5.8	0.67	5.8	0.67
501 - 1000	7	4948.66	2.71	0.79	8.51	1.46
1001 – 1500	14	17385.51	5.41	2.76	13.92	4.22
1501 – 2000	36	63267.69	13.89	10.06	27.81	14.28
2001 – 2500	64	145821.75	24.71	23.18	52.52	37.46
2501 – 3000	46	126591.71	17.76	20.13	70.28	57.59
3001 – 3500	51	164756.93	19.69	26.19	89.97	83.78
3501 – 4000	18	66037.48	6.95	10.51	96.92	94.29
4000 and above	8	35998.24	3.08	5.71	100	100

Sources: Field Survey 2005-06.

Table 5.4 (b)
Distribution of calorie intake among the population of Middle range

Calorie group	*Total number of person (F)*	*Total calorie intake (Q)*	*% of F*	*% of Q*	*Cf of F*	*Cf of Q*
0 – 500	1	0	1.25	0	1.25	0
501 - 1000	6	5078.29	7.5	2.58	8.75	2.58
1001 – 1500	5	6328.23	6.25	3.22	15	5.8
1501 – 2000	8	14470.32	10	7.35	25	13.15
2001 – 2500	16	37126.37	20	18.87	45	32.02
2501 – 3000	23	61411.92	28.75	31.22	73.75	63.24
3001 – 3500	13	42663.49	16.25	21.69	90	84.93
3501 – 4000	7	25547.04	8.75	12.99	98.75	97.92
4000 and above	1	4089.5	1.25	2.08	100	100

Sources: Field Survey 2005-06.

Table 5.4 (c)
Distribution of calorie intake among the population of Lower range

Calorie group	*Total number of person (F)*	*Total calorie intake (Q)*	*% of F*	*% of Q*	*Cf of F*	*Cf of Q*
0 – 500	1	0	1.9	0	1.9	0
501 - 1000	1	826.08	1.9	0.62	3.8	0.62
1001 – 1500	3	4053.72	5.6	3.02	9.4	3.64
1501 – 2000	12	21953.09	22.2	16.38	31.6	20.02
2001 – 2500	12	27038.97	22.2	20.19	53.8	40.21
2501 – 3000	17	48432.51	31.4	36.16	85.2	76.37
3001 – 3500	0	0	0	0	85.2	76.37
3501 – 4000	6	21734.54	11.1	16.23	96.3	92.6
4000 and above	2	9912.92	3.7	7.4	100	100

Sources: Field Survey 2005-06.

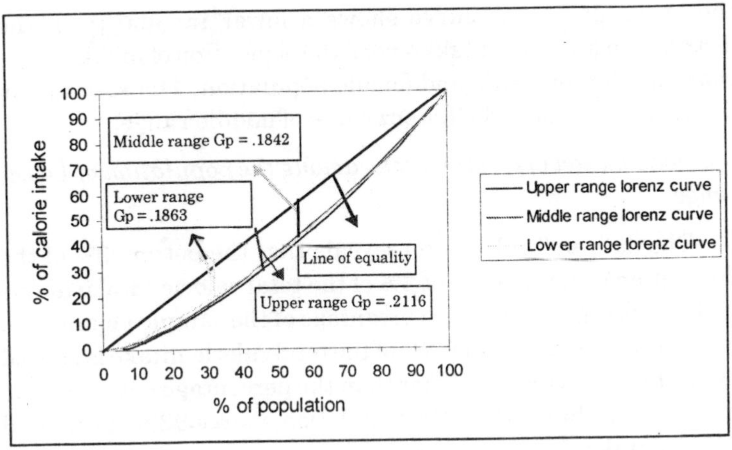

Figure 21: Range-wise distribution of calorie intake.

(b) Distribution of calorie intake among the population of middle range

The data in Table 5.4 (b) reveals that the bottom 15% of the population consumes only 5.8% of the total calorie intake at one end that is higher than the percentage of the sample population. But at the other end about 15% of the total calorie intake is shared by the top 10%, which is slightly lower than the percentage of the sample population. Thus 90% of the populations share 85% of the total calorie intake.

The value of Gini-coefficient (Gp) for calorie intake among the population of middle range has been worked as follows:

$$\text{Gini Coefficient (Gp)} = \frac{\text{Area between Lorenz Curve and Diagonal(G)}}{\text{Total Area under Diagonal}}$$

$$Gp = \frac{28848.91 - 27007.36}{100 \text{ X } 100}$$

$$Gp = .1842.$$

The value of Gini-coefficient of calorie intake for the population of middle range comes out to be .1842. Both Gini-coefficients and the shape of Lorenz curve shows a lower inequality in the distribution of calorie intake among the population of middle range than the sample, male and female population. The rose line in figure 21 represents the Lorenz curve of middle range.

(c): Distribution of calorie intake among the population of Lower range

The data in Table 5.4 (c) reveals that the bottom 9% of the population consumes about 3% of the total calorie intake at one end that is higher than the percentage of the sample population. But at the other end about 7% of the total calorie intake is shared by the top 3%, which is higher than the percentage of the sample population. Thus 96% of the population shares 92% of the total calorie intake.

The value of Gini-coefficient (Gp) for calorie intake among the population of lower range has been worked following the formulas:

$$\text{Gini Coefficient (Gp)} = \frac{\text{Area between Lorenz Curve and Diagonal}}{\text{Total Area under Diagonal}}$$

$$Gp = \frac{29608.78 - 27744.98}{100 \text{ X } 100}$$

$$Gp = .1863.$$

The value of Gini-coefficient of calorie intake for the population of lower range has been worked out at .1863. Both the Gini-coefficients and the shape of Lorenz curve shows a higher inequality in the distribution of calorie intake among the population of lower range than middle range but lower inequalities than the sample, male and female population. The yellow line in figure 21 represents the Lorenz curve of lower range.

(v) Distribution of calorie intake according to Sex-wise head of the household

The cumulated percentages among the population of male and female headed family as well as their daily calorie intake are presented in Table 5.5 (a and b). The cumulated percentages calorie intake and population of male and female headed family, when plotted on a graph paper gives the resultant shape which is evident from figure 22.

Table 5.5 (a)
Distribution of calorie intake among the population of Male-headed family

Calorie group	*Total number of person (F)*	*Total calorie intake (Q)*	*% of F*	*% of Q*	*Cf of F*	*Cf of Q*
0 – 500	14	3117.4	4.48	0.42	4.48	0.42
501 - 1000	15	11385.32	4.79	1.52	9.27	1.94
1001 – 1500	18	22976.48	5.75	3.06	15.02	5
1501 – 2000	48	85667.21	15.34	11.4	30.36	16.4
2001 – 2500	72	166171.56	23	22.12	53.36	38.52
2501 – 3000	69	189984.76	22.04	25.29	75.4	63.81
3001 – 3500	46	149579.54	14.69	19.91	90.09	83.72
3501 – 4000	23	84445.21	7.35	11.24	97.44	94.96
4000 and above	8	37846.03	2.56	5.04	100	100

Sources: Field Survey 2005-06.

Table 5.5 (b)
Distribution of calorie intake among the population of Female-headed family

Calorie group	*Total number of person (F)*	*Total calorie intake (Q)*	*% of F*	*% of Q*	*Cf of F*	*Cf of Q*
0 – 500	2	549.64	2.5	0.27	2.5	0.27
501 - 1000	0	0	0	0	2.5	0.27
1001 – 1500	4	4790.98	5	2.29	7.5	2.56
1501 – 2000	8	14023.89	10	6.73	17.5	9.29
2001 – 2500	21	46389.79	26.25	22.25	43.75	31.54
2501 – 3000	17	46629.71	21.25	22.34	65	53.88
3001 – 3500	17	55088.29	21.25	26.43	86.25	80.31
3501 – 4000	8	28873.85	10	13.85	96.25	94.16
4000 and above	3	12154.63	3.75	5.84	100	100

Sources: Field Survey 2005-06.

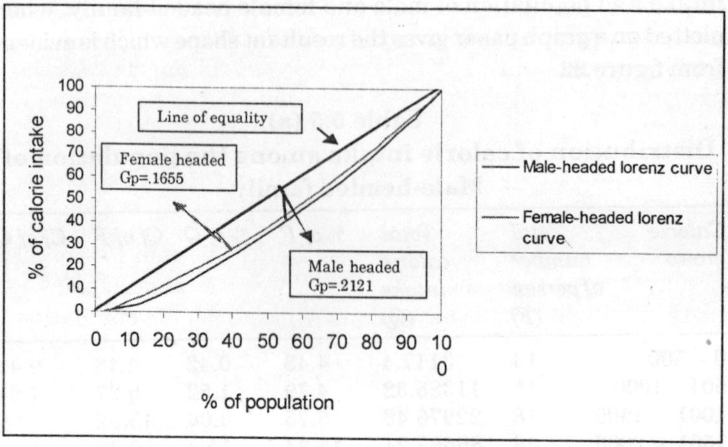

Figure 22: Sex-wise head of the household distribution of calorie intake

(a) Distribution of calorie intake among the population of Male-headed family

The data in Table 5.5 (a) reveals that the bottom 15% of the population consumes about 5% of the total calorie intake at one end that is higher than the percentage of the sample population. But at the other end about 16% of the total calorie intake is shared by the top 10%, which is slightly lower than the percentage of the sample population. Thus 90% of the population share 83% of the total calorie intake, quite similar with that of the sample population.

The value of Gini-coefficient (Gp) for calorie intake among the population of male-headed family has been worked following the formulas:

$$\text{Gini Coefficient (Gp)} = \frac{\text{Area between Lorenz Curve and Diagonal}}{\text{Total Area under Diagonal}}$$

$$Gp = \frac{29487.17 - 27366.66}{100 \text{ X } 100}$$

$$Gp = .2121.$$

The value of Gini-coefficient of calorie intake for the population of male-headed family has been worked out at .2121. Both the

Gini-coefficients and the shape of Lorenz curve shows a higher inequality in the distribution of calorie intake among the population of male-headed family than the sample population. The Lorenz curve of male headed family is represented by the blue line in figure 22.

(b) Distribution of calorie intake among the population of Female-headed family

The data in Table 5.5 (b) reveals that the bottom 17% of the population consumes about 9% of the total calorie intake at one end that is higher than the percentage of the sample population. But at the other end about 19% of the total calorie intake is shared by the top 13%, which is lower than the percentage of the sample population. Thus 86% of the population share 80% of the total calorie intake, which is lower than the sample population.

The value of Gini-coefficient (Gp) for calorie intake among the population of female-headed family has been worked following the formulas:

$$\text{Gini Coefficient (Gp)} = \frac{\text{Area between Lorenz Curve and Diagonal}}{\text{Total Area under Diagonal}}$$

$$Gp = \frac{25952.4 - 24297.03}{100 \text{ X } 100}$$

$$Gp = .1655.$$

The value of Gini-coefficient of calorie intake for the population of female-headed family comes out to be .1655. Both Gini-coefficient and the shape of Lorenz curve shows the lower inequalities in the distribution of calorie intake among the population of female-headed family as compared to that of the sample population and male headed family. The Lorenz curve of female headed family is represented by the pink line in figure 22.

(vi) Distribution of calorie intake according to Occupation-wise head of the household

The cumulated percentages among the population of service and agricultural headed households and their daily calorie intake are presented in Table 5.6 (a and b). The cumulated percentages calorie intake and population of the service and agricultural headed household, when plotted on a graph paper gives the resultant shape which is evident from figure 23.

Table 5.6 (a)

Distribution of calorie intake among the population of Service headed households

Calorie group	*Total number of person (F)*	*Total calorie intake (Q)*	*% of F*	*% of Q*	*Cf of F*	*Cf of Q*
0 – 500	4	970.2	2.52	0.26	2.52	0.26
501 - 1000	5	2704.8	3.14	0.72	5.66	0.99
1001 – 1500	10	12846.61	6.29	3.46	11.95	4.45
1501 – 2000	22	39666.55	13.84	10.69	25.79	15.14
2001 – 2500	42	95522.79	26.42	25.73	52.20	40.87
2501 – 3000	34	93875.15	21.38	25.29	73.58	66.16
3001 – 3500	36	115973.9	22.64	31.24	96.23	97.40
3501 – 4000	4	1499.31	2.52	0.40	98.74	97.80
4000 and above	2	8162.27	1.26	2.20	100	100

Sources: Field Survey 2005-06.

Table 5.6 (b)

Distribution of calorie intake among the population of Agricultural headed households

Calorie group	*Total number of person (F)*	*Total calorie intake (Q)*	*% of F*	*% of Q*	*Cf of F*	*Cf of Q*
0 – 500	11	2147.2	4.7	0.38	4.7	0.38
501 - 1000	11	8230.1	4.7	1.44	9.4	1.82
1001 – 1500	12	14920.85	5.13	2.62	14.53	4.44
1501 – 2000	34	60024.55	14.53	10.52	29.06	14.96
2001 – 2500	51	116603.5	21.79	20.44	50.85	35.4
2501 – 3000	55	150078	23.5	26.31	74.35	61.71
3001 – 3500	25	81783.34	10.69	14.34	85.04	76.05
3501 – 4000	26	94751.25	11.11	16.61	96.15	92.66
4000 and above	9	41838.39	3.85	7.34	100	100

Sources: Field Survey 2005-06.

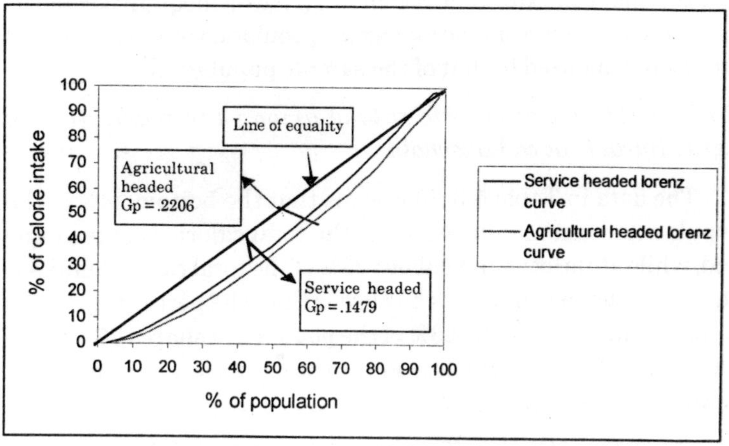

Figure 23: Occupation-wise distribution of calorie intake

(a) Distribution of calorie intake among the population of Service headed household

The data in Table 5.6 (a) reveals that the bottom 11% of the population consumes about 4% of the total calorie intake at one end, while at the other end about 33% of the total calorie intake is shared by the top 26%, which is lower than the percentage of the sample population. Thus 73% of the population shares 66% of the total calorie intake, which is lower than the sample population share.

The value of Gini-coefficient (Gp) for calorie intake among the population of service-headed family has been worked as follows:

$$\text{Gini Coefficient (Gp)} = \frac{\text{Area between Lorenz Curve and Diagonal}}{\text{Total Area under Diagonal}}$$

$$Gp = \frac{31168.18 - 29689.44}{100 \text{ X } 100}$$

Gp = .1479.

The value of Gini-coefficient of calorie intake for the population of service-headed family comes out to be .1479. Both Gini-coefficient and the shape of Lorenz curve shows a lower inequalities in the distribution of calorie intake among the population of service-headed family as compared to that of the sample population.

(b) Distribution of calorie intake among the population of Agricultural headed household

The data in Table 5.6 (b) reveals that the bottom 14% of the population consumes about 4% of the total calorie intake at one end, while at the other end about 23% of the total calorie intake is shared by the top 14%, which is lower than the percentage of the sample population. Thus 86% of the population shares 77% of the total calorie intake, which is lower than the sample population share.

The value of Gini-coefficient (Gp) for calorie intake among the population of agricultural-headed family has been worked as follows:

$$\text{Gini Coefficient (Gp)} = \frac{\text{Area between Lorenz Curve and Diagonal}}{\text{Total Area under Diagonal}}$$

$$\text{Gp} = \frac{27583.46 - 25377.77}{100 \text{ X } 100}$$

$$\text{Gp} = .2206.$$

The value of Gini-coefficient of calorie intake for the population of agricultural-headed family comes out to be .2206. Both Gini-coefficient and the shape of Lorenz curve show a higher inequality in the distribution of calorie intake among the population of agricultural-headed family as compared to that of the service-headed family and sample population. The pink line in figure 23 represents the Lorenz curve of agricultural headed family.

Measuring Inequality Through MPCE

Inequalities in the distribution of Monthly Per Capita Expenditure are being measured for different selected categories.

(i) Distribution of MPCE among the sample population

The cumulated percentages of the sample population as well as per capita monthly expenditure are presented in Table 5.7 (i). The cumulated percentages MPCE and population, when plotted on a graph paper gives the resultant shape, which is evident from figure 24. This figure reveals that the bottom 10% of the population is sharing about 6% of the total income at one end and at the other end about 13% of the total income is shared by the top 8% of the population. Thus 91% of the population shares 86% of the total income.

Table 5.7 (i)

Distribution of MPCE among the sample population

MPCE group	*Total number of person (F)*	*Total MPCE (Rs.)*	*% of person (F)*	*% of MPCE Q*	*Cf of F*	*Cf of Q*
0 - 600	13	7162.92	3.31	1.95	3.31	1.95
601 - 700	29	18909.17	7.38	5.21	10.69	7.16
701 - 800	61	45624.89	15.52	12.55	26.21	19.71
801 - 900	117	91387.27	29.77	25.56	55.98	45.27
901 - 1000	40	37909.83	10.18	10.24	66.16	55.51
1001 - 1100	45	47951.45	11.45	13.2	77.61	68.71
1101 - 1200	25	28737.51	6.36	7.9	83.97	76.61
1201 - 1300	29	35660.92	7.38	9.82	91.35	86.43
1301 - 1400	9	11953	2.29	3.2	93.64	89.63
1401 - 1500	16	23051.17	4.07	6.3	97.71	95.93
1500 and above	9	14792.46	2.29	4.07	100	100

Sources: Field Survey 2005-06.

The value of Gini-coefficient (Gp) for MPCE among the sample population has been worked with the help of the following formulas:

$$\text{Gini Coefficient (Gp)} = \frac{\text{Area between Lorenz Curve and Diagonal}}{\text{Total Area under Diagonal}}$$

Area between Lorenz Curve and Diagonal (G) is given by:

$$G = \sum_{i+1}^{n-1} (F_i Q_{i+1} - F_{i+1} Q_1)$$

$$Gp = \frac{49219.04 - 47827.02}{100 \text{ X } 100}$$

$$Gp = .1392.$$

The value of Gini-coefficient (Gp) for monthly per capita expenditure among the sample population has been worked out as .1392. Both the value of Gini-coefficient and the shape of Lorenz curve shows less inequalities in the distribution of income among the sample population as compared with that of the distribution in calorie intake.

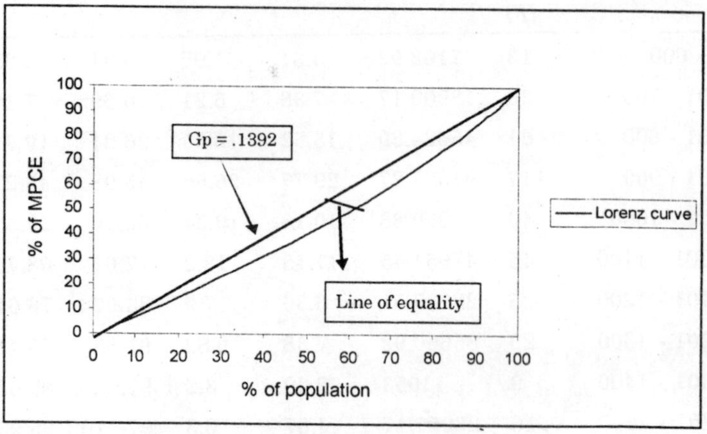

Figure 24: Distribution of MPCE among the Sample population

(ii) Gender-wise distribution of MPCE

The cumulated percentages among male and female population as well as their per capita monthly expenditure are presented in Tables 5.7 (ii, a and b). The cumulated percentages MPCE and male and female population, when plotted on a graph paper gives the resultant shape, which is evident from figure 25.

(a) Distribution of MPCE among the Male population

The data in Table 5.7 (ii, a) reveals that the bottom 10% of the population is sharing about 7% of the total income at one end, which is higher than the sample population average. However at the other end, about 9% of the total income is shared by the top 5% of the population that is lower than the share of the sample population. Thus 95% of the population share 91% of the total income that is higher than the sample population percentage.

The value of Gini-coefficient (Gp) for MPCE among the male population has been worked as follows:

$$\text{Gini Coefficient (Gp)} = \frac{\text{Area between Lorenz Curve and Diagonal}}{\text{Total Area under Diagonal}}$$

$$Gp = \frac{50321.42 - 49040.93}{100 \times 100}$$

$$Gp = .1280.$$

The value of Gini-coefficient (Gp) for monthly per capita expenditure among the male population has been worked out as .1280. Both the value of Gini-coefficient and the shape of Lorenz curve shows less inequalities in the distribution of income among the male population as compared to sample and female population.

5.7 (ii, a)

Distribution of MPCE among the male population

MPCE group	*Total number of person (F)*	*Total MPCE (Rs.)*	*% of person (F)*	*% of MPCE Q*	*Cf of F*	*Cf of Q*
1	*2*	*3*	*4*	*5*	*6*	*7*
0 - 600	3	1665.34	1.74	1.03	1.74	1.03
601 - 700	15	9823.57		8.726.09	10.46	7.12
701 - 800	27	20103.46	15.70	12.47	26.16	19.59

(Contd...)

1	*2*	*3*	*4*	*5*	*6*	*7*
801 - 900	56	47390.03	32.56	29.4	57.72	48.99
901 - 1000	17	15989.22	9.88	9.92	68.61	58.81
1001 - 1100	16	17095	9.3	10.6	77.91	69.41
1101 - 1200	12	13805.34	6.97	8.57	84.88	77.98
1201 - 1300	13	15942.12	7.56	9.89	92.44	87.87
1301 - 1400	3	3999.4	1.74	2.48	94.18	90.35
1401 - 1500	6	8609.42	3.49	5.35	97.67	95.7
1500 and above	4	6743.41	2.33	4. 3	100	100

Sources: Field Survey 2005-06.

Table 5.7 (ii, b)

Distribution of MPCE among the female population

MPCE group	*Total number of person (F)*	*Total MPCE (Rs.)*	*% of person (F)*	*% of MPCE Q*	*Cf of F*	*Cf of Q*
0 - 600	10	5497.58	4.52	2.63	4.52	2.63
601 - 700	14	9085.31	6.33	4.35	10.85	6.98
701 - 800	34	25521.42	15.39	12.22	26.24	19.20
801 - 900	61	51320.08	27.60	24.57	53.84	43.77
901 - 1000	27	25558.28	12.22	12.24	66.06	56.01
1001 - 1100	25	26758.71	11.31	12.81	77.37	68.82
1101 - 1200	13	14932.17	5.88	7.15	83.25	75.97
1201 - 1300	16	19718.8	7.24	9.45	90.49	85.42
1301 - 1400	6	7953.6	2.72	3.8 1	93.21	89.23
1401 - 1500	10	14441.76	4.52	6.92	97.73	96.14
1500 and above	5	8049.05	2.27	3.86	100	100

Sources: Field Survey 2005-06.

(b) Distribution of MPCE among the Female population

The data in Table 5.7 (ii, b) reveals that the bottom 10% of the population is sharing about 6% of the total income at one end, which is higher than the sample population average. However at the other end, about 10% of the total income is shared by the top 6% of the population that is higher than the share of the sample population. Thus 94% of the population share 90% of the total income that is higher than the sample population percentage.

The value of Gini-coefficient (Gp) for MPCE among the female population has been worked as follows:

$$\text{Gini Coefficient (Gp)} = \frac{\text{Area between Lorenz Curve and Diagonal}}{\text{Total Area under Diagonal}}$$

$$Gp = \frac{48747.87 - 47370.6}{100 \text{ X } 100}$$

$$Gp = .1377.$$

The value of Gini-coefficient (Gp) for monthly per capita expenditure among the female population has been worked out as .1377. Both the value of Gini-coefficient and the shape of Lorenz curve show higher inequalities in the distribution of income among the female population than male population but lower than sample population.

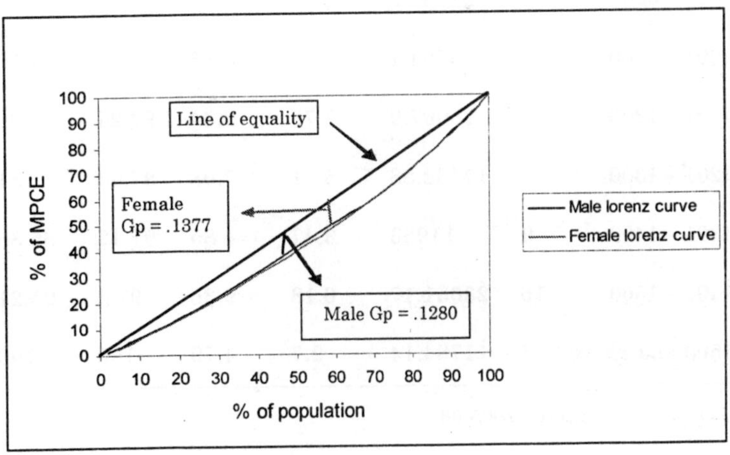

Figure 25: Gender-wise distribution of MPCE.

(iii) Village-wise distribution of MPCE

Village-wise distribution of MPCE is shown in Table 5.7 (iii, a, b, c and d). The cumulated percentages MPCE and population of these villages, when plotted on a graph paper gives the resultant shape, which is evident from figure 26.

Table 5.7 (iii, a)

Distribution of MPCE among the population of Longsa village

MPCE group	*Total number of person (F)*	*Total PCTE (Rs.)*	*% of person (F)*	*% of MPCE Q*	*Cf of F*	*Cf of Q*
0 - 600	13	7162.92	5.02	2.91	5.02	2.91
601 - 700	19	12326.17	7.33	5.01	12.35	7.92
701 - 800	38	28536.45	14.67	11.58	27.02	19.5
801 - 900	75	62463.94	28.96	25.36	55.98	44.86
901 - 1000	23	21762.2	8.89	8.84	64.87	53.7
1001 - 1100	25	26784.1	9.65	10.88	74.52	64.58
1101 - 1200	20	23007.9	7.72	9.34	82.24	73.92
1201 - 1300	14	17432.58	5.41	7.08	87.65	81
1301 - 1400	9	11953	3.47	4.85	91.12	85.85
1401 - 1500	16	23051.17	6.18	9.36	97.3	95.21
1500 and above	7	11784.14	2.7	4.79	100	100

Sources: Field Survey 2005-06.

Table 5.7 (iii, b)
Distribution of MPCE among the population of Yunchuchu village

MPCE group	*Total number of person (F)*	*Total MPCE (Rs.)*	*% of person (F)*	*% of MPCE Q*	*Cf of F*	*Cf of Q*
0 - 600	0	0	0	0	0	0
601 - 700	0	0	0	0	0	0
701 - 800	14	10466.35	33.33	27.46	33.33	27.46
801 - 900	10	8687	23.81	22.79	57.14	50.25
901 - 1000	7	6605.66	16.67	17.33	73.81	67.58
1001 - 1100	7	7526.01	16.67	19.75	90.48	87.33
1101 - 1200	0	0	0	0	90.48	87.33
1201 and above	4	4828.67	9.52	12.67	100	100

Sources: Field Survey 2005-06.

Table 5.7 (iii, c)
Distribution of MPCE among the population of Sunglup village

MPCE group	*Total number of person (F)*	*Total MPCE (Rs.)*	*% of person (F)*	*% of MPCE Q*	*Cf of F*	*Cf of Q*
0 - 600	0	0	0	0	0	0
601 - 700	0	0	0	0	0	0
701 - 800	9	6622.09	23.68	19.2	23.68	19.2
801 - 900	15	13061.16	39.48	37.87	63.16	57.07
901 - 1000	10	9542	26.32	27.67	89.48	84.74
1001 - 1100	1	1090.67	2.63	3.16	92.11	87.9
1101 - 1200	1	1164.91	2.63	3.38	94.74	91.28
1201 - 1300	0	0	0	0	94.74	91.28
1301 - 1400	0	0	0	0	94.74	91.28
1401 - 1500	0	0	0	0	94.74	91.28
1500 and above	2	3008.34	5.26	8.72	100	100

Sources: Field Survey 2005-06.

Table 5.7 (iii, d)
Distribution of MPCE among the population of Bhandari village

MPCE group	*Total number of person (F)*	*Total MPCE (Rs.)*	*% of person (F)*	*% of MPCE Q*	*Cf of F*	*Cf of Q*
0 - 600	0	0	0	0	0	0
601 - 700	10	6583	18.52	12.87	18.52	12.87
701 - 800	0	0	0	0	18.52	12.87
801 - 900	17	14498	31.48	28.35	50	41.22
901 - 1000	4	3637.67	7.41	7.11	57.41	48.33
1001 - 1100	8	8453	14.81	16.53	72.22	64.86
1101 - 1200	4	4564.67	7.41	8.93	79.63	73.79
1201 and above 1300	11	13399.67	20.37	26.21	100	100

Sources: Field Survey 2005-06.

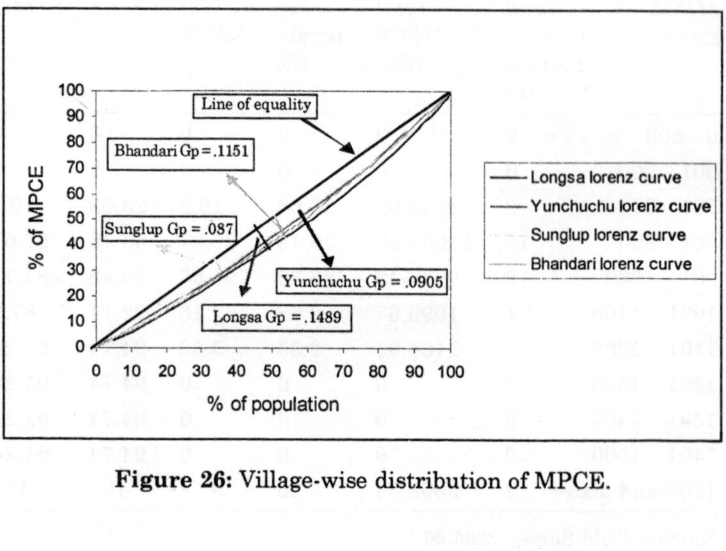

Figure 26: Village-wise distribution of MPCE.

(a) Distribution of MPCE among the population of Longsa village

The data in Table 5.7 (iii, a) reveals that the bottom 12% of the population is sharing about 7% of the total income at one end, which is lower than the sample population average. However at the other end, about 11% of the total income is shared by the top 8% of the population that is lower than the share of the sample population. Thus 91% of the population share 85% of the total income that is lower than the sample population percentage.

The value of Gini-coefficient (Gp) for MPCE among the population of Longsa has been worked as follows:

$$\text{Gini Coefficient (Gp)} = \frac{\text{Area between Lorenz Curve and Diagonal}}{\text{Total Area under Diagonal}}$$

$$Gp = \frac{46788.38 - 45298.41}{100 \text{ X } 100}$$

$$Gp = .1489.$$

The value of Gini-coefficient (Gp) for monthly per capita expenditure among the population of Longsa village has been worked out as .1489. Both the value of Gini-coefficient and the shape of Lorenz curve show higher inequalities in the distribution of income among the population of Longsa village than all other village and sample population.

(b) Distribution of MPCE among the population of Yunchuchu village

The data in Table 5.7 (iii, b) reveals that the bottom 33.33% of the population is sharing about 27% of the total income at one end, which is higher than the sample population share. However at the other end, about 12% of the total income is shared by the top 9% of the population that is lower than the share of the sample population. Thus 90% of the population share 87% of the total income that is higher than the sample population percentage.

The value of Gini-coefficient (Gp) for MPCE among the population of Yunchuchu has been worked as follows:

$$\text{Gini Coefficient (Gp)} = \frac{\text{Area between Lorenz Curve and Diagonal}}{\text{Total Area under Diagonal}}$$

$$Gp = \frac{28931.8 - 28027.27}{100 \text{ X } 100}$$

$$Gp = .0905.$$

The value of Gini-coefficient (Gp) for monthly per capita expenditure among the population of Yunchuchu village has been worked out as .0905. Both the value of Gini-coefficient and the shape of Lorenz curve show lower inequalities in the distribution of income among the population of Yunchuchu village than sample population.

(c) Distribution of MPCE among the population of Sunglup village

The data in table No. 5.2 (iii, c) reveals that the bottom 23.68% of the population is sharing about 19% of the total income at one end, which is higher than the sample population share. However at the other end, about 8% of the total income is shared by the top 5% of the population that is slightly lower than the share of the sample population. Thus 94% of the population share 91% of the total income that is higher than the sample population percentage.

The value of Gini-coefficient (Gp) for MPCE among the population of Sunglup has been worked as follows:

$$\text{Gini Coefficient (Gp)} = \frac{\text{Area between Lorenz Curve and Diagonal}}{\text{Total Area under Diagonal}}$$

$$Gp = \frac{58394.29 - 57523.94}{100 \text{ X } 100}$$

$$Gp = .0870.$$

The value of Gini-coefficient (Gp) for monthly per capita expenditure among the population of Sunglup village has been worked out as .0870. Both the value of Gini-coefficient and the shape of Lorenz curve show lower inequalities in the distribution of income among the population of Sunglup village than any other villages and the sample population.

(d) Distribution of MPCE among the population of Bhandari village

The data in Table 5.7 (iii, d) reveals that the bottom 18% of the population is sharing about 12% of the total income at one end, which is slightly higher than the sample population share. However at the other end, about 26% of the total income is shared by the top 20% of the population that is lower than the share of the sample population. Thus 79% of the population share 73% of the total income that is lower than the sample population percentage.

The value of Gini-coefficient (Gp) for MPCE among the population of Bhandari has been worked as follows:

$$\text{Gini Coefficient (Gp)} = \frac{\text{Area between Lorenz Curve and Diagonal}}{\text{Total Area under Diagonal}}$$

$$Gp = \frac{20433.97 - 19282.49}{100 \text{ X } 100}$$

$$Gp = .1151.$$

The value of Gini-coefficient (Gp) for monthly per capita expenditure among the population of Bhandari village has been worked out as .1151. Both the value of Gini-coefficient and the shape of Lorenz curve show lower inequalities in the distribution of income among the population of Bhandari village than the sample population.

(iv) Range-wise distribution of MPCE

Range-wise estimation of inequalities in the distribution of income/MPCE is shown in the Table 5.8 (a, b and c). The cumulated percentages of income and population of these ranges, when plotted on a graph paper gives the resultant shape which is evident from figure 27.

Table 5.8 (a)

Distribution of MPCE among the population of Upper range

MPCE group	*Total number of person (F)*	*Total MPCE (Rs.)*	*% of person (F)*	*% of MPCE Q*	*Cf of F*	*Cf of Q*
0 - 600	13	7162.92	5.02	2.91	5.02	2.91
601 - 700	19	12326.17	7.33	5.01	12.35	7.92
701 - 800	38	28536.45	14.67	11.58	27.02	19.5
801 - 900	75	62463.94	28.96	25.36	55.98	44.86
901 - 1000	23	21762.2	8.89	8.84	64.87	53.7
1001 - 1100	25	26784.1	9.65	10.88	74.52	64.58
1101 - 1200	20	23007.9	7.72	9.34	82.24	73.92
1201 - 1300	14	17432.58	5.41	7.08	87.65	81
1301 - 1400	9	11953	3.47	4.85	91.12	85.85
1401 - 1500	16	23051.17	6.18	9.36	97.3	95.21
1500 and above	7	11784.14	2.7	4.79	100	100

Sources: Field Survey 2005-06

Table 5.8 (b)
Distribution of MPCE among the population of Middle range

MPCE group	*Total number of person (F)*	*Total MPCE (Rs.)*	*% of person (F)*	*% of MPCE Q*	*Cf of F*	*Cf of Q*
0 - 600	0	0	0	0	0	0
601 - 700	0	0	0	0	0	0
701 - 800	23	17088.44	28.75	23.54	28.75	23.54
801 - 900	25	21748.16	31.25	29.95	60	53.49
901 - 1000	17	16147.66	21.25	22.24	81.25	75.73
1001 - 1100	8	8616.68	10	11.87	91.25	87.60
1101 - 1200	1	1164.91	1.25	1.60	92.5	89.20
1201 - 1300	4	4828.67	5	6.65	97.5	95.85
1301 - 1400	0	0	0	0	97.5	95.85
1401 - 1500	0	0	0	0	97.5	95.85
1500 and above	2	3008.34	2.5	4.15	100	100

Sources: Field Survey 2005-06.

Table 5.8 (c)
Distribution of MPCE among the population of Lower range

MPCE group	*Total number of person (F)*	*Total MPCE (Rs.)*	*% of person (F)*	*% of MPCE Q*	*Cf of F*	*Cf of Q*
0 - 600	0	0	0	0	0	0
601 - 700	10	6583	18.52	12.87	18.52	12.87
701 - 800	0	0	0	0	18.52	12.87
801 - 900	17	14498	31.48	28.35	50	41.22
901 - 1000	4	3637.67	7.41	7.11	57.41	48.33
1001 - 1100	8	8453	14.81	16.53	72.22	64.86
1101 - 1200	4	4564.67	7.41	8.93	79.63	73.79
1201 and above 1300	11	13399.67	20.37	26.21	100	100

Sources: Field Survey 2005-06.

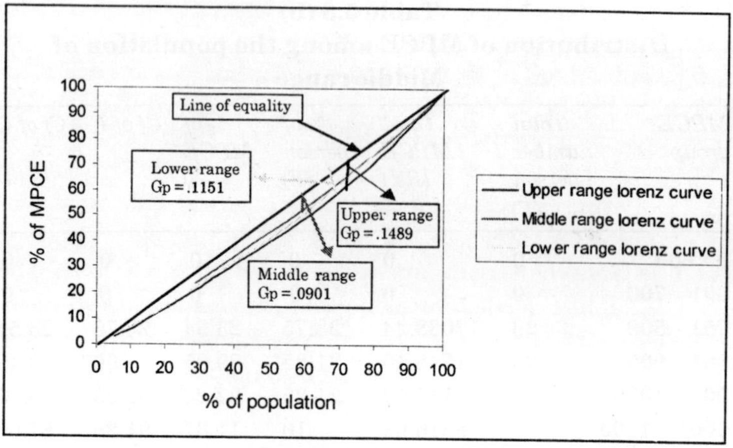

Figure 27: Range-wise distribution of MPCE.

(a) Distribution of MPCE among the population of Upper range

The data in Table 5.8 (a) reveals that the bottom 12% of the population is sharing about 7% of the total income at one end, which is lower than the sample population average. However at the other end, about 11% of the total income is shared by the top 8% of the population that is lower than the share of the sample population. Thus 91% of the population share 85% of the total income that is lower than the sample population percentage.

The value of Gini-coefficient (Gp) for MPCE among the population of upper range has been worked as follows:

$$\text{Gini Coefficient (Gp)} = \frac{\text{Area between Lorenz Curve and Diagonal}}{\text{Total Area under Diagonal}}$$

$$\text{Gp} = \frac{46788.38 - 45298.41}{100 \text{ X } 100}$$

$$\text{Gp} = .1489.$$

The value of Gini-coefficient (Gp) for monthly per capita expenditure among the population of upper range has been worked out as .1489. Both the value of Gini-coefficient and the shape of Lorenz curve show higher inequalities in the distribution of income among the population of upper range than all the other range and sample population.

(b) Distribution of MPCE among the population of Middle range

The data in Table 5.8 (b) reveals that the bottom 28.75% of the population is sharing about 23.54% of the total income at one end that is higher than the percentage of the sample population. But at the other end about 10% of the total income is shared by the top 7%, which is slightly lower than the percentage of the sample population. Thus 93% of the population shares 90% of the total income.

The value of Gini-coefficient (Gp) for MPCE among the population of middle range has been worked as follows:

$$\text{Gini Coefficient (Gp)} = \frac{\text{Area between Lorenz Curve and Diagonal}}{\text{Total Area under Diagonal}}$$

$$\text{Gp} = \frac{58645.51 - 57744.58}{100 \text{ X } 100}$$

$$\text{Gp} = .0901.$$

The value of Gini-coefficient (Gp) for monthly per capita expenditure among the population of middle range has been worked out as .0901. Both the value of Gini-coefficient and the shape of Lorenz curve show lower inequalities in the distribution of income among the population of middle range than all the other range and sample population.

(c) Distribution of MPCE among the population of Lower range

The data in Table 5.8 (c) reveals that the bottom 18% of the population is sharing about 12% of the total income at one end, which is slightly higher than the sample population share. However at the other end, about 26% of the total income is shared by the top 20% of the population that is lower than the share of the sample population. Thus 79% of the population share 73% of the total income that is lower than the sample population percentage.

The value of Gini-coefficient (Gp) for MPCE among the population of Lower range has been worked as follows:

$$\text{Gini Coefficient (Gp)} = \frac{\text{Area between Lorenz Curve and Diagonal}}{\text{Total Area under Diagonal}}$$

$$Gp = \frac{20433.97 - 19282.49}{100 \text{ X } 100}$$

$$Gp = .1151.$$

The value of Gini-coefficient (Gp) for monthly per capita expenditure among the population of lower range has been worked out as .1151. Both the value of Gini-coefficient and the shape of Lorenz curve show lower inequalities in the distribution of income among the population of lower range than the sample population.

(v) Distribution of MPCE according to Sex-wise head of the household

Sex-wise head of the household estimation of inequalities in the distribution of income/MPCE is shown in the Table 5.9 (a and b). The cumulated percentages of income and population of these ranges, when plotted on a graph paper gives the resultant shape which is evident from figure 28.

Table 5.9 (a)

Distribution of MPCE among the population of male headed family

MPCE group	*Total number of person (F)*	*Total MPCE (Rs.)*	*% of person (F)*	*% of MPCE Q*	*Cf of F*	*Cf of Q*
0 - 600	11	6184.83	3.51	2.08	3.51	2.08
601 - 700	19	12326.2	6.07	4.16	9.58	6.24
701 - 800	52	38747.8	16.62	13.09	26.2	19.33
801 - 900	88	74265.6	28.12	25.08	54.32	44.41
901 - 1000	37	34839.5	11.82	11.77	66.14	56.18
1001 - 1100	32	34152.1	10.22	11.54	76.36	67.72
1101 - 1200	22	25310.1	7.03	8.56	83.39	76.28
1201 - 1300	24	29245.4	7.67	9.88	91.06	86.16
1301 - 1400	7	9324	2.24	3.15	93.3	89.31
1401 - 1500	16	23051.2	5.11	7.79	98.41	97.1
1500 and above	5	8571.4	1.59	2.9	100	100

Sources: Field Survey 2005-06.

Table 5.9 (b)

Distribution of MPCE among the population of Female headed family

MPCE group	*Total number of person (F)*	*Total MPCE (Rs.)*	*% of person (F)*	*% of MPCE Q*	*Cf of F*	*Cf of Q*
0 - 600	2	978.09	2.5	1.32	2.5	1.32
601 - 700	10	6583	12.5	8.9	15	10.22
701 - 800	9	6877.14	11.25	9.3	26.25	19.52
801 - 900	29	24444.55	36.25	33.04	62.5	52.56
901 - 1000	7	6708	8.75	9.07	71.25	61.63
1001 - 1100	9	9701.68	11.25	13.11	82.5	74.74
1101 - 1200	3	3427.4	3.75	4.63	86.25	79.37
1201 - 1300	5	6415.5	6.25	8.67	92.5	88.04
1301 - 1400	2	2629	2.5	3.55	95	91.59
1401 - 1500	0	0	0	0	95	91.59
1500 and above	4	6221.06	.5	8.41	100	100

Sources: Field Survey 2005-06.

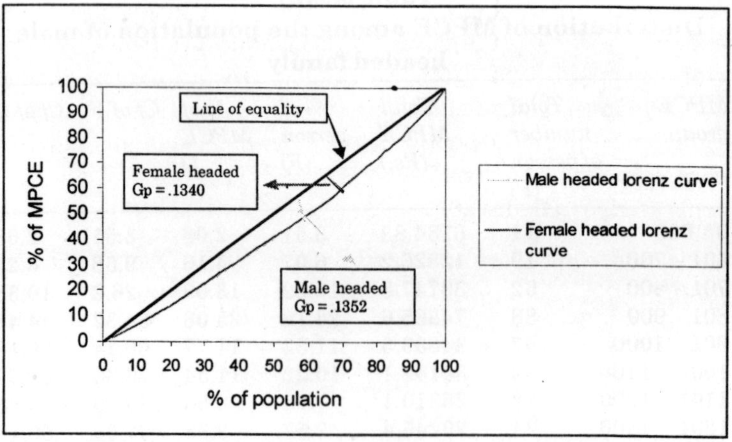

Figure 28: Sex-wise head of the household distribution of MPCE.

(a) Distribution of MPCE among the population of Male headed family

The data in Table 5.9 (a) reveals that the bottom 9% of the population is sharing about 6% of the total income at one end, which is slightly higher than the sample population share. However at the other end, about 10% of the total income is shared by the top 6% of the population that is slightly higher than the share of the sample population. Thus 94% of the population share 90% of the total income that is higher than the sample population percentage.

The value of Gini-coefficient (Gp) for MPCE among the population of male-headed family has been worked as follows:

$$\text{Gini Coefficient (Gp)} = \frac{\text{Area between Lorenz Curve and Diagonal}}{\text{Total Area under Diagonal}}$$

$$\text{Gp} = \frac{48943.95 - 47591.55}{100 \text{ X } 100}$$

Gp = .1352.

The value of Gini-coefficient (Gp) for monthly per capita expenditure among the population of male-headed family has been worked out as .1352. Both the value of Gini-coefficient and the shape of Lorenz curve show lower inequalities in the distribution of income among the population of male-headed family than the sample population. The Lorenz curve of male headed family is represented in figure 28.

(b) Distribution of MPCE among the population of female headed family

The data in Table 5.9 (b) reveals that the bottom 15% of the population is sharing about 10% of the total income at one end, which is higher than the sample population share. However at the other end, about 11% of the total income is shared by the top 7% of the population that is lower than the share of the sample population. Thus 95% of the population shares 91% of the total income that is slightly higher than the sample population percentage.

The value of Gini-coefficient (Gp) for MPCE among the population of female-headed family has been worked as follows:

$$\text{Gini Coefficient (Gp)} = \frac{\text{Area between Lorenz Curve and Diagonal}}{\text{Total Area under Diagonal}}$$

$$Gp = \frac{51689.75 - 50349.35}{100 \text{ X } 100}$$

$$Gp = .1340.$$

The value of Gini-coefficient (Gp) for monthly per capita expenditure among the population of female-headed family has been worked out as .1340. Both the value of Gini-coefficient and the shape of Lorenz curve show lower inequalities in the distribution of income among the population of female-headed family than the sample population. The Lorenz curve of female headed family is represented in figure 28.

(vi) Distribution of MPCE according to Occupation-wise head of the household

The cumulated percentages among the population of service and agriculturalist headed family as well as their per capita monthly expenditure are presented in Table 5.10 (a and b). The cumulated percentages MPCE and population of service and agriculturalist headed family, when plotted on a graph paper gives the resultant shape which is evident from figure 29.

(a) Distribution of MPCE among the population of service headed family

The data in Table 5.10 (a) reveals that the bottom 9% of the population is sharing about 6% of the total income at one end, which is higher than the sample population share. However at the other end, about 14% of the total income is shared by the top 10% of the population that is lower than the share of the sample population. Thus 90% of the population shares 86% of the total income that is slightly higher than the sample population percentage.

The value of Gini-coefficient (Gp) for MPCE among the population of service-headed family has been worked as follows:

$$\text{Gini Coefficient (Gp)} = \frac{\text{Area between Lorenz Curve and Diagonal}}{\text{Total Area under Diagonal}}$$

$$Gp = \frac{51494.32 - 50483.96}{100 \text{ X } 100}$$

$$Gp = .1011.$$

The value of Gini-coefficient (Gp) for monthly per capita expenditure among the population of service-headed family has been worked out as .1011. Both the value of Gini-coefficient and the shape of Lorenz curve show lower inequalities in the distribution of income among the population of service-headed family than the sample population but higher than agriculturalist.

Table 5.10 (a)

Distribution of MPCE among the population of Service headed family

MPCE group	*Total number of person (F)*	*Total MPCE (Rs.)*	*% of person (F)*	*% of MPCE Q*	*Cf of F*	*Cf of Q*
0 - 600	0	0	0	0	0	0
601 - 700	15	10069	9.43	6.46	9.43	6.46
701 - 800	17	13025.07	10.69	8.36	20.12	14.82
801 - 900	42	38798.91	26.42	24.89	46.54	39.71
901 - 1000	21	19985.17	13.21	12.82	59.75	52.53
1001 - 1100	32	34240.94	20.13	21.96	79.88	74.49
1101 - 1200	15	17200.1	9.43	11.03	89.31	85.52
1201 - 1300	10	12266.25	6.29	7.87	95.6	93.39
1301 - 1400	0	0	0	0	95.6	93.39
1401 - 1500	7	10303.83	4.40	6.61	100	100
1500 and above	0	0	0	0	100	100

Sources: Field Survey 2005-06.

Table 5.10 (b)

Distribution of MPCE among the population of Agricultural headed family

MPCE group	*Total number of person (F)*	*Total MPCE (Rs.)*	*% of person (F)*	*% of MPCE Q*	*Cf of F*	*Cf of Q*
0 - 600	13	7162.9	5.56	3.54	5.56	3.54
601 - 700	14	8840.2	5.98	4.37	11.54	7.91
701 - 800	44	32599.8	18.8	16.1	30.34	24.01
801 - 900	78	65474.25	33.33	32.35	63.68	56.36
901 - 1000	23	21562.33	9.82	10.65	73.50	67.01
1001 - 1100	9	9612.84	3.85	4.75	77.35	71.76
1101 - 1200	9	10398.25	3.85	5.14	81.20	76.9
1201 - 1300	19	23394.7	8.12	11.56	89.32	88.46
1301 - 1400	10	1392.16	4.27	0.69	93.59	89.15
1401 - 1500	9	12745.3	3.85	6.3	97.44	95.45
1500 and above	6	9229.4	2.56	4.55	100	100

Sources: Field Survey 2005-06.

(b): Distribution of MPCE among the population of Agricultural headed family

The data in Table 5.10 (b) reveals that the bottom 11% of the population is sharing about 7% of the total income at one end, which is higher than the sample population share. However at the other end, about 10% of the total income is shared by the top 6% of the population that is higher than the share of the sample population. Thus 94% of the population shares 90% of the total income that is slightly higher than the sample population percentage.

The value of Gini-coefficient (Gp) for MPCE among the population of agricultural-headed family has been worked as follows:

$$\text{Gini Coefficient (Gp)} = \frac{\text{Area between Lorenz Curve and Diagonal}}{\text{Total Area under Diagonal}}$$

$$Gp = \frac{51343.78 - 50341.85}{100 \times 100}$$

$$Gp = .1001.$$

The value of Gini-coefficient (Gp) for monthly per capita expenditure among the population of agricultural-headed family has been worked out as .1001. Both the value of Gini-coefficient and the shape of Lorenz curve show lower inequalities in the distribution of income among the population of agricultural-headed family than the sample population.

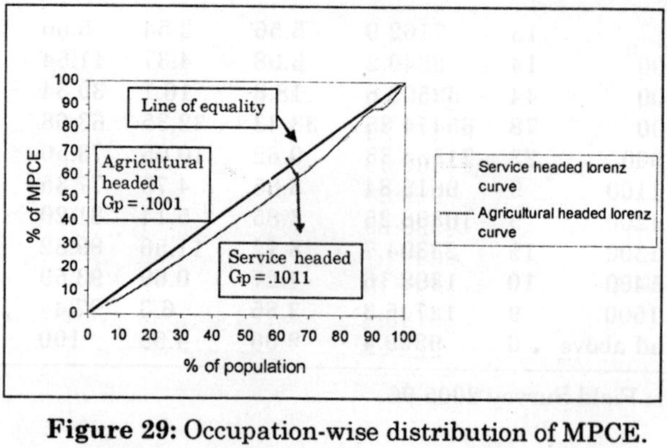

Figure 29: Occupation-wise distribution of MPCE.

Inequality in the Distribution of Calorie Intake and the Proportion of Poor

To estimate the relationship that existed between the inequalities in the distribution of calorie intake and the proportion of poor we look at the Gini-coefficients in the distribution of calorie intake and the Head Count Ratio measured using the sample survey calorie norms as given in Table 5.11.

Table 5.11
Gini-coefficient and the Head Count Ratio of Calorie intake

Selected category	*Gini-coefficients*	*HCR (Measured using sample survey norms)*
Sample population	.2032	.4606
Gender-wise		
Male	.2067	.4826
Female	.1996	.4479
Village-wise		
Longsa	.2116	.4633
Yunchuchu	.2235	.5476
Sunglup	.0984	.2895
Bhandari	.1863	.4815
Range-wise		
Upper	.2116	.4633
Middle	.1840	.45
Lower	.1863	.4815
Sex-wise Head of the Household		
Male headed family	.2121	.4601
Female headed family	.1655	.4375
Occupation-wise Head of the Household		
Service	.1479	.4654
Agriculture	.2206	.4531

Source: Field Survey 2005-06.

Looking at the correlation between the distribution of calorie intake and the proportion of poor measured through the sample survey norms, it was found that the correlation coefficient value is positive (r = 0.79). Testing the significance of the relation, it was also found that the positive correlation coefficient is significant as its r value is more than ten times greater than its probable error of 0.068. To test whether the correlation is significant or otherwise, t-test is undertaken. It was found that the calculated value of t is 15.456 which is very much higher than the table value of t (= 1.782). Since the calculated value is higher than the table value, the correlation is significant at 5% level for 12 degrees of freedom. Therefore, the hypothesis is accepted. Hence higher the inequality in the distribution of calorie intake higher will be the proportion of poor. The effect on proportion of poor from a change in the distribution of calorie intake has been analysed through simple regression method.

$$Y = .2 + 1.227X$$

Where, y is the proportion of poor and x is the inequality in the distribution of calorie intake. This result shows that the regression coefficient 'byx' of Y on X is 1.277. The positive value of the regression coefficient indicates that the relation between y and x is direct. This shows that a unit change in the distribution of calorie intake (X) will have an impact on the proportion of poor (Y) by 1.277 times. To see whether the regression analysis is significant or not, t-test is undertaken. The result shows that the calculated value of t (t = 2.446) is much higher than the table value ($t_{0.05}$ = 1.782), therefore, the value of b is significant at 5% level for 12 degrees of freedom. Hence a small change in the distribution of calorie intake will have a large positive impact on the proportion of poor.

Inequality in the Distribution of MPCE and the Proportion of Poor

To estimate the relationship that existed between the inequalities in the distribution of calorie intake and the proportion of poor we look at the Gini-coefficients in the distribution of MPCE and the Head Count Ratio measured using the sample poverty line as given in Table 5.12.

Table No. 5.12
Gini-coefficient and the Head Count Ratio of MPCE

Selected category	*Gini-coefficients*	*Sample survey poverty line*
Sample population	.1392	.5954
Gender-wise		
Male	.1280	.6279
Female	.1377	.5701
Village-wise		
Longsa	.1489	.5792
Yunchuchu	.0905	.5714
Sunglup	.0870	.7632
Bhandari	.1151	.5741
Range-wise		
Upper	.1489	.5792
Middle	.0901	.6625
Lower	.1151	.5741
Sex-wise Head of the Household		
Male headed family	.1352	.5879
Female headed family	.1340	.625
Occupation-wise Head of the Household		
Service	.1011	.4969
Agriculture	.1001	.6752

Source: Field Survey 2005-06.

The correlation coefficient value of inequality and the proportion of poor shows a negative relation (- 0.386). To test whether the correlation is significant or otherwise, t-test is undertaken. It was found that the calculated value of t ($|t| = 1.346$) is lower higher than the table value of t ($|t| = 1.782$). Since the calculated value is lower than the table value, the correlation is not significant at 5% level for 12 degrees of freedom. Therefore, the hypothesis which states that higher the disparity in the distribution of income/MPCE, higher will be the proportion is rejected.

From the analysis of inequalities among the selected category, the following conclusion may be drawn:

1) The extent of inequality in terms of calorie intake is higher among the sample population than measured in terms of the MPCE.

2) Gender-wise, the degree of inequality is higher among the male than female in terms of calorie intake and vice-versa in terms of MPCE.

3) Among the sample villages, Yunchuchu exhibits highest degree of inequality in terms of calorie intake, while Longsa shows the highest inequality in terms of MPCE.

4) A range-wise inequality shows that upper range exhibits the highest degree of inequality both in terms of calorie intake and MPCE.

5) Sex-wise head of the household shows that the extent of inequality is higher among the male headed households than female headed households both in terms of calorie intake and MPCE.

6) It also reveals from the analysis among the occupation-wise head of the household, the inequalities in terms of calorie intake is higher among the agricultural headed families while in terms of MPCE it is the service headed households.

7) Higher the inequality in the distribution of calorie intake higher will be the proportion of poor.

6

Findings and Conclusions

Although at the national level estimation of poverty have been done in general yet no detail and comprehensive studies had so far been conducted on the estimation of poverty and inequalities among the rural population of Nagaland both at the national as well as at the state level. Thus, the basic objective of this research was to estimate poverty and inequalities of the rural people of Nagaland. The extent of poor amongst the sample population have been derived based on both sample norms and compared it with the NSSO norms of the State and Country. Then the extent of inequalities in the distribution of calorie intake and income (MPCE) that existed among the rural population are also examined in detail. Moreover, the levels of different socio-economic indicators of the study area, which have direct bearing on poverty of the rural population have been empirically analysed. The important findings of the study are highlighted in this chapter.

Socio-economic Indicators

In chapter 2 the socio-economic characteristic were discussed in detail. Here are the salient findings.

(i) The indicators of demographic characteristics show that Wokha district has the highest decennial population growth rate with 95.01% as against the state growth rate of 69.44% in 2001. In Wokha the average household size is 6.23 persons, which is higher than the state average of 6.1 persons in 2001. Further, based on the data collected from the respective village councils of the sample villages; it was found that the average household size is 7.44 persons.

However, based on the sample household data, the average household size is 3.97 persons only. Thus there is no conformity in the data relating to household size. If we accept the estimated household size generated from the present sample household data, it may be inferred that the high population growth rate of the district as indicated by 2001 census may be an exaggerated figure which requires a separate in-depth study.

(ii) A distinctive demographic characteristics that emerge from the study is, the proportion of female population are significantly higher than the male population, which differs from the State's and the Country's sex ratio. This fact has been confirmed by the households sample data estimates of 1284 female per 1000 males.

(iii) The household data reveals that the literacy rate is 73.25%, which is lower than the district literacy rate of 81.28% but higher than the state literacy rate of 67.11%. Gender-wise analysis shows that male has higher literacy rate of 83.92% than female with 64.48%.

(iv) The development of educational infrastructure in the sample villages is far from satisfactory. Altogether, there are 8 schools ranging from primary to middle school levels. The teacher-student ratio for the sample village is 1: 10, which is better than the district and the state ratio of 1:20 and 1: 21 respectively.

(v) In regard to the availability of public health care facilities, each sample village has 1 dispensary that caters to the health care need of the people. Further, on an average 1 medical personal (Nurses/compounders) serves 809.44 people which is better than the district ratio of 1:947.63

and state ratio of 1: 945.17. However, it was found that none of the dispensary is looked after by doctors.

(vii) Among the many basic needs for human well-being, housing and sanitation facility are of vital importance. The study reveals that none of the population is without shelter. However, the quality of housing differs among the households. On an average, only 6.06% of the households reside in pucca house, which is lower than the district average of 18.90%. While the households residing in semi-pucca houses account for 27.27%, which is lower than the district average of 59.06%. This implies that majority of the households reside in Kutcha houses (66.67%).

Further, only 29.29% of the sample household has proper sanitation as against 63.38% of the district and 57% of the state averages. This implies that more than two-third of the households live in poor quality house with inadequate sanitation.

(vi) Although the government report shows that 82.17% of the villages in Wokha district have been provided with safe drinking water supply facility, yet none of the sample villages has tap water connectivity. Thus, people of these villages depend entirely on wells, brooks and rain to meet the domestic needs of water.

(viii) Electricity is equally important for the well-being of the people. The household survey indicates that 79.79% of the households have electricity connectivity. Yet this is lower than both the districts and the states rural household electrification percentage of 93.75% and 93.89% respectively. Thus, 20% of the households in the sample villages are still without these basic facilities. There is a wide variation among the sample villages in this respect. Yunchuchu village reveals that 88.89% households have been electrified, whereas, in Sunglup only 50% households have been electrified.

(ix) All weather road connectivity is the basic need to improve the living conditions of the rural population. However, it is discouraging to observe that except for Longsa all other villages are covered by Kutcha roads. For Wokha district, only 17.05% of the villages are linked by pucca road which is below the state percentage of 23.61%.

(x) The result of the analysis on banking and post office indicates that there are no branches or sub-office in of the sample villages. Moreover, no telephone connectivity was found in any of the sample household.

(xi) The analysis on the sectoral employment among the sample household reveals that 60.08% of the total work force are engaged in agriculture which is lower than the district average of 66.06% and the state average of 68.03% as well. Moreover, all the sample households are partly or fully engaged in jhum cultivation which is the most primitive method of cultivation with low income potential. 25.29% of the total workforce is engaged in service but none of the households are engaged in industrial activities.

The Estimated Calorie Intake

The result of cross section assessment of the average calorie intake per person per day by age group, village, gender, sex-wise and occupation-wise head of the households as discussed in chapter 3 shows the following result.

(i) On an average, the per capita calorie intake is estimated at 2441.92 Kcal for the sample population. This average is higher than the NSSO estimate for the National and State rural areas by 19.29% and 19.47% respectively.

(ii) The age-wise average calorie intake shows that it increases from age 1 year and less to 40-49 years, thereafter it declines because of the obvious reason.

(iii) The average calorie intake per person per day among the female population is 2453.16 Kcal that is marginally higher than the male population average of 2427.48 Kcal by 1.06%.

(iv) Among the villages Sunglup and Bhandari with an average of 2613.65 Kcal and 2480.59 Kcal, respectively, are higher than the sample average (2441.92 Kcal) by 7.03% and 1.58% respectively. On the other hand, Longsa and Yunchuchu villages with an average calorie intake of 2428.59 Kcal and 2318.97 Kcal respectively, are lower than the sample average by .55% and 5.03% respectively.

(v) Range-wise calorie intake shows that the average calorie intake is highest in Lower range with 2480.59 Kcal per person per day. For middle range the average calorie intake is 2458.94 Kcal per person per day. However, Upper range with an average calorie intake of 2428.59 Kcal exhibits the lowest average calorie intake.

(vi) The per capita calorie intake per day by the sex-wise head of household shows that the calorie intake of female-headed households is 2582.31 Kcal, which is higher than male headed households of 2455.2 Kcal by 9.78%.

(vii) The estimates of the calorie intake by the occupation-wise head of the household reveals that households headed by farmers have higher averages of 2582.31 Kcal per person per day than the service headed household of 2455.2 Kcal per person per day.

The Estimated Monthly Per Capita Expenditur (MPCE)

The assessment of the average monthly per capita expenditure (MPCE) by village, gender, sex-wise head and occupation-wise head of the household has been discussed in depth in chapter 3. Following are the most important findings.

(i) On an average, the monthly per capita expenditure for the sample population is Rs. 942.66 Rs. 942.66 or Rs. 31.42 per person per day at 2005-06 prices, which is higher than the NSSO estimation for National rural average by 69% but lower than State rural averages by 7%. The food items accounts for 77% while non-food items account for 23% of the total monthly per capita expenditure (MPCE).

(ii) The village-wise result shows that Longsa has the highest average MPCE of Rs 950.18 per month or Rs. 31.67 per person per day at 2005-06 prices followed by Yunchuchu has an average MPCE of Rs 844.82 per month or Rs. 28.16 per person per day at 2005-06 prices, Sunglup has an average MPCE of Rs 866.82 per month or Rs. 28.89 per person per day at 2005-06 prices and Bhandari has an average MPCE of Rs 920.48 per month or Rs. 30.68 per person per day at 2005-06 prices.

(iii) The range-wise average MPCE assessment shows that Upper range has an average MPCE of Rs 950.18 per month or Rs. 31.67 per person per day at 2005-06 prices while Middle range has an average MPCE of Rs 907.54 per month or Rs. 30.25 per person per day at 2005-06 prices and Lower range has an average MPCE of Rs 920.48 per month or Rs. 30.68 per person per day at 2005-06 prices.

(iv) The sex-wise head of the households analysis reveals that the average MPCE of male headed households is Rs. 945.74 or Rs. 31.52 per person per day at 2005-06 prices, while it is Rs. 924.82 or Rs. 30.83 per person per day at 2005-06 prices with female headed households. This may be due to higher income earning opportunities for male, which leads to higher income resulting in higher MPCE for male headed households. Moreover, the proportions of monthly expenditure on food items reveals that female headed households spend a greater proportion of their expenditure is made on food items as compared to male headed households. It may be due to the reason that when women have sole control over family resources, the expenditure on food items tend to be higher because they are more concern in providing better food to the family.

The analysis on occupation-wise head of the household shows that the average MPCE of service headed households is Rs. 999.41 or Rs. 33.31 per month per person at 2005-06 prices. While the average MPCE of agricultural headed households with Rs. 961.12 or 32.04 per person per day at 2005-06 prices.

Estimation of Relationship

In chapter 3 the relationship between the per capita calorie intake per day with the size of the family, calorie intake and income/ MPCE and MPCE and family size have been examined. The result reveals the following relationship:

(i) The correlation coefficient between the average per capita per day calorie intake and family size shows that there exist a negative relationship (r = -0.703). The correlation between the two variables was tested to be significant since the calculated value of t is higher than the table value of t. Thus, the hypothesis which states that higher the family size lower the average calorie intake is accepted. The reason for lower average calorie intake in higher family size is due to the existence of higher number of children.

(ii) The value of correlation between per capita calorie intake and per capita monthly income is closer to 0 (.0089), therefore there is no linear relationship between the variables.

However, the information about the monthly income as provided by the interviewee cannot be considered as reliable because of two reasons. Firstly, people in the rural areas does not keep any record of their monthly income, thus reliable data at the household level is not available. Secondly, people seldom tell their true monthly income to any interviewer. Therefore, Per Capita Monthly Expenditure is used as a proxy of income while measuring poverty. The Report of the Expert Group (1993) maintains that the household consumer expenditure is more reliable than income and hence more suitable for measuring poverty. The reliability of the consumption expenditure is well recognized.[1]

(iii) The value of correlation between MPCE and average calorie intake per day, it was found that the correlation coefficient is 0.94. Since the calculated value of t is much higher than the table value of t, the correlation is significant. Therefore, the hypothesis is accepted. Hence people with higher monthly MPCE consumes higher calorie.

(iv) The correlation coefficient between the family size and MPCE shows a negative relation (r = -0.57). The correlation between the two variables was tested to be significant since the calculated value of t is higher than the table value of t. Thus the hypothesis which states that higher the family size lower will be the average MPCE is accepted. The reason for lower average MPCE in higher family size is due to the existence of higher number of children.

(v) The correlation between the distribution of calorie intake and the proportion of poor measured through the sample survey norms, it was found that the correlation coefficient value is positive (r = 0.79). The positive correlation coefficient was proved to be significant as the calculated value of t is very much higher than the table value of t. Thus the hypothesis which states that higher the inequality in the distribution of calorie intake, higher will be the proportion of poor is accepted.

(vi) The correlation coefficient value of inequality in the distribution of MPCE and the proportion of poor shows a negative relation (- 0.386). However, it was found that the correlation is not significant since the calculated value of t is lower higher than the table value of t. Therefore, the hypothesis is rejected.

Estimation of Poverty

1. Estimating Through Calorie Norms

The result of poverty measurement based on different calorie norms for the selected category has been explained in detail in chapter 4. The salient findings are:

(i) *Sample population*: The result on the estimation of Head Count Ratio (HCR) based on National and State rural nutritional norms shows that 28.75% of the sample population are poor or are living below the calorie norms.

Whereas, the HCR based on sample survey norms show a higher percentage of poor for the sample population with 46.06%.

For the calorie gap ratio based on National norms, the result came out to be 10.01% per poor person for the sample population. This means that every poor person is falling short of the calorie norm by 204.9 Kcal. However, calorie gap ratio based on State norms shows a lower percentage of 9.97% per poor person for the sample population. Whereas, the calorie gap ratio based on Sample survey norms shows a higher calorie deprivation for the sample population with 14.49% per poor person. It means to help every poor person at the calorie norms, calorie intake of 353.83 Kcal per poor person is required.

The result also shows that Sen Index (P) based on National norms is 7.65% for the sample population. It implies that 7.65% of poor amongst the poor are falling below their calorie norm (mean calorie intake of the poor). Whereas, Sen Index based on State norms is 7.64% for the sample population. However, the P based on Sample norms shows that the extent calorie deprivation is higher for the sample population with 11.59% of poor amongst the poor falling below their calorie norm.

The estimated result of Foster, Greer and Thorbecke (P^F) based on National norms shows that the severity of calorie deprivation for the sample population is 5.92% for the poorest of the poor. This means that 5.92% of the poorest of the poor are far below the calorie norms. Whereas, P^F based on State norms cutoff is 5.91% for the sample population. It means that 5.91% of the poorest of the poor are far below the calorie norms. However, the P^F based on Sample norms shows that calorie inadequacy is more severe for the sample population with 7.79% for the poorest of the poor.

(ii) *Gender-wise:* The estimates of poverty based on both NSSO and sample explains that the incidence, depth and severity of calorie deprivation falls more on male than female.

(iii) *Village-wise:* The comparison among different villages on the incidence of poverty based on NSSO calorie norms reveals that Bhandari has the highest proportion of poor (31.48%). But when it is measured based on sample survey calorie norms, Yunchuchu stands the highest (54.76%). On the other hand Sunglup is placed at the bottom of the ranking under both calorie norms. Based on all calorie norms, it is seen that the depth and severity of calorie deprivation is the highest in Yunchuchu and lowest in Sunglup.

(iv) *Range-wise:* The range-wise estimates on poverty showed that the proportion of poor is highest in lower range across different calorie norms. However, the depth and severity of calorie deprivation is highest in upper range across different calorie norms. But the Sen Index of calorie deprivation is highest in middle range across different calorie norms.

(V) *Sex-wise head of household:* The estimates of poverty on sex-wise head of the households reveal that the proportion, depth, sensitivity and severity of calorie inadequacy falls more on male headed households across different calorie norms.

(vi) *Occupation-wise head of household:* The comparison between service and agricultural headed households in the proportion and severity of calorie deprivation based on NSSO calorie norms reveals that the proportion and percentage of the poorest poor is higher in agricultural headed household than the service headed households. However, the depth and sensitivity of calorie deprivation based on NSSO and sample survey calorie norms reveals that it is higher in agricultural headed households than the service headed household.

2. Estimating Through MPCE

The result of poverty measurement based on different poverty line for the selected category has been discussed in detailed in chapter 4. The salient findings are given below.

(i) *Sample population:* The result of Head Count Ratio (HCR) based on National rural poverty line shows that 2.04% of the sample population is poor. The HCR based on State rural poverty line shows that 67.18% of the sample populations are poor. However, the HCR based on Sample poverty line reveals that 59.54% of the sample populations are poor which is higher than the proportion of poor for the rural Nagaland as shown by the Planning Commission in 1999-2000 as 40.04%.

The analysis of poverty gap ratio based on National poverty line for the sample population is .13% per poor person. This means that every poor person is falling short of the income by Rs. 0.73. In other words, to support every poor person at the poverty line, Rs. 0.72 of income is needed per poor person. The poverty Gap ratio based on State poverty line shows a higher income deprivation for the sample population with 13.82%. However, the poverty gap ratio based on sample poverty line with 10.09% shows a lower income deprivation for the sample population than the estimation based on State poverty line but higher than the estimation based on National poverty line.

The result on the estimation of Sen Index (P) based on National poverty line reveals that 0.11% of poor amongst the poor in the sample population are falling below their poverty line. The P based on the State poverty line shows that the extent of income deprivation for the sample population is 21.22%. However, the P based on sample poverty line shows that 16.94% of poor amongst the poor are living below the mean income of the poor.

The analysis of Foster, Greer and Thorbecke measure (P^F) based on National poverty line shows that 0.01% of the poorest poor are facing income inadequacy. The P^F based on the State poverty line shows that 5.22% of the poorest of the poor are far below the poverty line. However, the P^F based on sample poverty line shows that income inadequacy with 4.2% for the poorest poor is less severe than the estimation based on State poverty line but more severe than the estimation based on National poverty line.

On comparison between the estimate based on state poverty line and sample survey poverty line, it was found that the proportion, depth and severity based on State poverty line are higher.

(ii) *Gender-wise:* The gender-wise estimation of poor based on National poverty line shows that the incidence and depth of income deprivation of female is higher among male. However, the estimation based on State and sample survey poverty line reveals that the incidence and depth of male poor is higher than female poor. The comparison between male and female P^F based on NSSO and sample poverty line shows that the income inadequacy of female is higher than male.

(iii) *Village-wise:* The village-wise estimation on poor based on National poverty line shows that the proportion of poor is higher in Longsa. However, the proportion of poor is shown highest in Sunglup when the estimation if based on Sample and State poverty line. The estimation of depth of poverty based on National shows that Bhandari has the highest shortfall of income, while Longsa exhibit the highest when the estimation is based on National and sample survey poverty line. However, the sensitivity measures based on National and sample poverty line shows that Longsa has the highest number of poor who are falling below their average poverty norm. However, the estimate based on State poverty line shows that Sunglup has the number of poor who are falling below their average poverty norm. The severity of income based on NSSO and sample survey poverty line shows that Longsa has the highest income inadequacy among the sample villages.

(iv) *Range-wise:* Range-wise estimation based on National poverty line shows that the proportion, depth and severity of poor exist only in upper range, while other ranges shows that every one is above the poverty line. The poverty gap ratio estimates based on State poverty line shows that among the ranges the highest depth of income deprivation exists in lower range. However, the estimation of poverty gap ratio based on sample poverty line indicates that upper range has the highest shortfall of income per person. The estimation of Sen Index (P) based on State poverty line and sample survey poverty line shows that middle range has the highest number of poor amongst the poor. Range-wise analysis of P^F based on state and sample poverty line shows that upper range has the highest severity of income deprivation.

(v) *Sex-wise head of household:* The estimation of poor based on NSSO and sample poverty line reveals that the proportion of poor, depth and severity of poverty is higher in female headed family than male headed. It may be due to the fact that the income earning ability of male is higher than female.

(vi) *Occupation-wise head of household:* The result of poverty estimation based on National poverty line shows that the proportion, depth and severity of poor among agricultural headed households is higher than the service headed households. However, the estimate based on the State poverty line reveals that the proportion of poor is higher in service headed households than agricultural headed households. The estimation based on State and sample poverty line shows that the depth and severity of income inadequacy is higher in among agricultural headed households than the service headed households.

Estimation of Inequalities

1. Estimating Through Calorie Intake

(i) *Sample population:* The distribution of calorie intake among the population reveals that the bottom 14% of the population consumes about 4% of the total calorie intake at one end and at the other end about 17% of the total calorie intake is shared by the top 10%. Thus 90% of the population share 83% of the total calorie intake. This shows that the distribution of calorie intake is not fairly equal. This is confirmed by the Gini index or coefficient of .2032.

(ii) *Gender-wise:* Both Gini-coefficient (.1996) and the cumulative distribution of calorie intake shows more equitable distribution of calorie intake among the population of female as compared to that of the sample and male population.

(iii) *Village-wise:* The cumulated percentages of calorie intake and Gini-coefficient (.0984) among the population of Sunglup village show that it has the lowest percentage of inequalities as compared to other villages.

(iv) *Range-wise:* Both Gini-coefficient and the shape of Lorenz curve shows lower inequalities in the distribution of calorie intake among the population of middle range as compared to that of the sample population and the other two ranges.

(v) *Sex-wise head of household:* Both Gini-coefficient (.1655) and the distribution of calorie intake shows lower inequalities among the population of female-headed family as compared to that of the sample population and male headed family.

(vi) *Occupation-wise head of household:* The distribution of calorie intake among the service headed households and the Gini-coefficient (.1479) of service headed households exhibits the existence of lower inequalities.

2. Estimating Through Income/MPCE

(i) *Sample population:* The distribution of income among the sample population reveals that the bottom 10% shares about 6% of the total income at one end and at the other end about 13% of the total income is shared by the top 8% of the population. This shows that there exist inequalities in the distribution of income among the sample population and the Gini-coefficient of income distribution is .1392.

(ii) *Gender-wise:* Both Gini-coefficient (.1280) and the distribution of income show less inequalities in the distribution of income among male population than the sample population but higher than the female.

(iii) *Village-wise:* The distribution of income/MPCE and the Gini-coefficient (.0870) in Sunglup village show less inequalities compared to other villages and the sample population.

(iv) *Range-wise:* Both Gini-coefficient and the shape of Lorenz curve shows the lower inequalities in the distribution of income among the population of middle range as compared to that of the other two ranges.

(v) *Sex-wise head of household:* The distribution of income and the Gini-coefficient (.1340) confirms that there exist a lesser inequalities among the female headed family than male headed family.

(vi) *Occupation-wise head of household*: Both the Gini-coefficient (.1001) and the distribution of income shows lower inequalities among the agricultural headed family than service headed family.

Poverty Alleiation Programme

The result of the analysis on the impact of poverty alleviation programme on the sample population reveals that only 4.07% of the total sample populations have been benefited from the implementation of poverty alleviation programme. Out of this 1.78% of the population got the help from JRY, while 2.29% of the population got the Below Poverty Line (Rice). Among the villages, 5.79% of the populations in Longsa were benefited from the implementation of poverty alleviation programme. Out of this, 2.32% benefited from JRY, while 3.47% benefited from the Below Poverty Line (Rice). Sunglup followed next with 2.63% of its total population surveyed getting the benefits from JRY. For the remaining two villages surveyed showed a zero benefit from any such programmes by the sample population. The resultant figure clearly reveals that only a meagre proportion of poor of the sample population have been benefited from such programmes, while

64.64% (based on State Poverty line) of the poor or 57.73% (based on Sample survey poverty line) of the poor remained outside the parameter of the poverty alleviation programme. This clearly shows the failure of the poverty alleviation programme in giving complete coverage to the poor people.

Policy Implication and Suggestion

Measurement of poverty has great bearing in resolving issues that arise for designing cost-effective relief work schemes especially on the aspects relating to choices of coverage for the scheme and choice for the benefit level.

(i) The existence of poverty line has significant bearing on the policy choice over coverage of poverty alleviation programmes, as it defines the critical income level needed to escape poverty in a given society and that attaining this income level is qualitatively significant. Therefore, Nagaland state can use the nutritional norms of 2441.92 Kcal per person per day and the poverty line of Rs. 942.60 per person per month or Rs. 31.42 per person per day (at 2005-06 prices) as the official norms and poverty line. The reason being that so far no scholars or the government agency (Economic and Statistics Department) in the state has ever come out with it. Moreover, the NSSO data cannot be trusted for the reason that those investigator posted in the state does the entire questionnaire at the desk.

(ii) Identifying the unique level of calorie intake by different age groups helps the policy maker to fight malnutrition in rural areas (especially the Social Welfare Department in the State). Therefore, the calorie intake for different age and sex group explained in chapter 3 can be used as the official norms for the state.

(iii) Head count index cannot be of much use when it comes to fighting poverty for the reason that it tells only the proportion of poor and nothing more. Therefore, while implementing any poverty alleviation programme, the Sen

Index and Foster, Greer and Thorbacke Indices should be taken into consideration, since these measures help the implementing agency to target the benefits towards the poorest of the poor.

(iv) It follows that systematic survey and assessment of actual status of the living standards must be undertaken before implementing any programmes meant for poverty alleviation, so as to device a programme which will ensure coverage, target, transfer and impact efficiencies with high benefit-cost ratio. Based on the estimation of the proportion of poor (HCR) and the measure of severity in income (MPCE) deprivation among the villages, it was found that even though Sunglup has the highest proportion of poor people, yet the severity of income among the poorest of the poor falls more in Longsa village. This implies that in order to achieve various efficiencies, while implementing any poverty alleviation programme, the severity of deprivation needs to be considered. Similarly, among the other selected categories, the most vulnerable sections were male, female-headed households and agricultural-headed households. Thus, these sections of population should be the targeted group under any poverty alleviation programme.

(v) Implementation of any poverty alleviation programme should be followed by the evaluation of the programme implementation to see who truly benefits. This will check the loopholes in achieving the targets as well as act as a deterrent to corruption practice.

(vi) In Nagaland it is a common affair for the implementing agencies in giving fake address to earn extra income. Therefore, while undertaking the evaluation project, the government should give the names and addresses of the beneficiaries to the evaluators. This will help the evaluators in getting the actual amount gone to the poor and the amount that were lost half way.

(vii) The sample survey shows that none of the household has been covered by the ongoing NREGA scheme. Therefore, it must be extended to all the rural areas targeting the poorest of the poor as it promotes supplementary employment for unskilled labour. This programme is self-selecting having target efficiency as the wages are low so as to attract the poorest of the poor. Under this programme, the benefit-cost ratio may not be so high, as its direct transfer of benefit to individuals is usually small, but the indirect benefit to the society as a whole will be huge.

(viii) Selection of any such programme must be directed towards providing indirect benefits to the poor from the assets created under the employment generation scheme. As such, assets created under the programme should be durable (not just for instance, roads that are washed away in the next rain) and should benefit the poor at least along with the non-poor, through growth, developing rural-urban linkages etc.

(ix) The programme like land development and conservation must be given importance as social security options because land provides food security enables utilization of family labour and reduces vulnerability of the poor in labour and food market.

(x) Availability of credit can also play important safety net function, which can prevent asset depletion of the poor and provide working capital to the self-employed poor.

(xi) The study reveals that the incidence of poverty and inequality are positively related in terms of calorie intake. This implies that higher equitable distribution of calorie intake leads to lower incidence of poverty in a given social strata. It underlines the need to pursue a specific policy with an objective to ensure equal access to food and nutrition. In view of this objective, public distribution system needs to be extended to the rural areas as this system ensures high transfer efficiency and wide coverage.

Also midday school meals and children nutrition schemes are viewed as a means to attain food security. Further, it has an indirect impact on improving school enrolment and attendance. Thus this programme needs to be more regular with improved quality of food.

(xii) The survey result shows that the social assistance programme for old age pension at present is Rs. 90 per month. This rate needs to be enhanced to a reasonable level so that it will help the beneficiaries in meeting the basic minimum needs.

a) This kind of social assistance should be extended to poor widows and handicaps.

b) Moreover, maternity assistance limiting to the first two births, equal to two or three months wages for the female agricultural labour may be given in the rural areas.

c) The selection of the beneficiaries should be based on distributionally sensitive measure of poverty, targeting the poorest of the poor. Such social assistance will benefit a very high proportion of the poor especially women who are in absolute destitution.

(xiii) The social assistance and poverty alleviation programmes should be operated through the decentralized delivery systems operating through local institutions in which poor are members and which system empowers them, so as to reduce the costs of information, check frauds and corruptions at the roots. This system also enables quick settlement of claims, localization, provisions of credits, etc.

(xiv) Training programme for the development of skills and technical know-how to the rural population is required so as to enhance their earning capacity and income.

(xv) Other indirect approaches to poverty alleviation programmes that are related to health and education policy like child care and nutrition can also influence nutritional status.

(xvi) To ensure a better standard of living for the rural population of Nagaland importance should be given to the development of physical and social infrastructures. The development of these infrastructures will indirectly uplift the living standard of the rural population.

a) The road connectivity to the rural areas should be an all weather road. This is important because it will improve transport and communication, which in turn will improve the connectivity to urban areas and thereby leads to better agricultural marketing system of the rural people.

b) Since 66.67% of the total households in the sample villages are still residing in Kutcha house and 70.71% rural households do not have proper sanitation facility. Therefore it may be suggested the ongoing programme that covers housing of the rural people should still be continued and implemented judiciously. Moreover, common toilets for male and female separately should be built in every rural village.

c) Safe drinking water supply by the government to every village has to be given priority.

d) The connectivity of electricity to every household coupled with regular power supply should be emphasized. This is vital for the growth of small scale and cottage industries.

e) At least one medical doctor should be placed in every village. This will save time, money and health of the rural population, which in turn will improve their productive capacity.

f) None of the households covered by the sample survey has telephone connectivity, thus, it may be suggested that this facility should be extended to them at a minimum rate.

g) More over, banking and post office branches should be extended to the rural areas.

h) Organization of Self Help Group in rural areas should be encouraged and strengthened. This is important because it will improve the business efficiency; develop leadership qualities and co-operative awareness among the rural masses.

i) Primary and Middle schools in the sample villages needs to be upgraded to high school level.

Conclusion

The present empirical study reveals that lots need to be done in development of credit, social securities and basic amenities like, housing, provision of potable water, health care facilities, proper road condition, education, subsidized food supplies and agriculture sector. This is important because it will improve the living condition of the rural people which will directly or indirectly reduce the proportion of poor. Moreover, there exists high percentage of poor population in the district as measured at both State (67.18%) as well as Sample survey poverty line (59.54%). The result also reveals that the income deprivation of the poor people is more than 10% per person measured using the state as well as sample survey poverty line. The severity of income deprivation comes out at more than 4% for the poorest poor estimated using the same poverty line. Thus, any policy designed to ameliorate the plight of the poor must, among other things, recognize the importance of these income deprivation and severity of the poor apart from the proportion of the poor, before implementing any anti-poverty programmes. This is vital for proper coverage and impact efficiency of any poverty alleviation programme. Thus, the need to alleviate poverty in Wokha in particular and Nagaland as a whole should be the highest priority of the government because no society can surely flourish when greater part of its population is poor and miserable. For which, proper assessment of the extent and severity of income deprivation is vital for implementing and targeting the beneficiaries. Moreover, the present administrative mechanism is not likely to be efficient for the task, therefore, local delivery system at grass root level should be involved and empowered.

NOTE

1. *Ibid.*, 39.

Bibliography

Ahluwalia, M.S. (1974), "Income Inequality: Some Dimensions of the Problem", *Finance and Development*, September 1974.

Ahmed, F. (2004), "Practices of Poverty Measurement and Poverty Profile of Bangladesh", *ERD Working Paper No. 54*, Asian Development Bank. Online [available] at www.povertymap.net 2004.

Ahuja, R. (1992), *Social Problems in India*, Rawat Publications, New Delhi, p.30.

Alam, A., Murthi, M., Yemtsov, R., Murrugarra, E., Dudwick, N., Hamilton, E., and Tiongson, E. (2005); "Growth, Poverty and Inequality: Eastern Europe and the Former Soviet Union", Europe and Central Asia Region, World bank .Online [available] at *www.worldbank.org*.

Anand, S. (2002); "The Definition and Measurement of Poverty", In Subramanian S (ed) 2002, *Measurement of Inequality and Poverty*, p.250.

Anand, S. (2002); "Measurement of Income Inequality", In Subramanian S. (ed) 2002, *Measurement of Inequality and Poverty*.

Ao, A. L., Sinha A. C. (Eds) (1993); *Rural Development In Nagaland*, Har-anand Publications, New Delhi.

Aturupane, H., Glewwe, P. and Isenman, P. (1994), "Poverty, Human Development and Growth: An emerging consensus?"

The American Economic Review, Vol. 84, Issue 2, Paper and Proceedings of the Hundred and Sixth Annual Meeting of the American Economic Association (May 1994), pp.244-49.

Bagchee, A. (2005), "Political and Administration Realities of Employment Guarantee Scheme", *Economic and Political Weekly*, Oct 15 issue 2005. Online [available] at www.epw.org.

Bardhan, P. D. (1970), "Green Revolution and Agriculture Labourers", *Economic and Political Weekly*, Vol. 5, No's, 29-30, July 1970 and vol. 5. No. 46, November 1970.

Bardhan, P. K. (1973), "On the Incidence of Poverty in Rural India", *Annual Number*, February 1973.

Barro, R. J. (1999), "Inequality and Growth in a Panel of Countries", Harvard University. Online [available] at *www.economics.harvard.edu.*

Becker, H. (1996), *Social Problems: A Modern Approach*, John Willy and Son Inc., New York, p.436.

Bhalla, S. S. (2003), "Recounting the Poor: Poverty in India, 1983-99" *Economic and Political Weekly*, Feburary 25, 2003, Vol. XXXVIII, pp.338-49.

Bhargava, A. (1997), "Nutritional Status and the Allocation of Time in Rwandese Households", *Journals of Econometrics*, Vol. 77, pp.277-95.

Bhargava, A. and Ravallion, M. (1993), "Does Household Behave as a Martingale? A Test for Rural South India", *The Review of Economics and Statistics*, Vol. 75, Issue 3, pp.500-04.

Bhatia, B.M. (1967). *Famines in India: A Study of Some Aspects of the Economic History of India (1860-1965)*, Asia Publishing House, London.

Behrman, J. R. and Deolalikar, A. (1987), "Will Developing Country Nutrition Improve with Income? A Case Study for Rural South India", *The Journal of Political Economy*, Vol. 95, Issue 3 (June 1987) pp.492-507.

Behrman, J. R. and Deolalikar, A. (1989), "Is Variety the Spice of Life? Implication for Calorie Intake", *The Review of Economics and Statistics*, Vol. 71, Issue 4, pp. 666-72.

Behrman, J. R., Foster, A. D. and Rosenzweig, M. R (1997), "The Dynamics of Agricultural Production and the Calorie-income Relationship; Evidence from Pakistan", *Journal of Econometrics*, Vol. 77, pp.187-207.

Behrman J.R., Alderman, H. and Hoddinott, J. (2004), "Hunger and Malnutrition", *Copenhagen Census Challenger Paper*, 7 May 2004, p.3.

Bernstein, J. and Sherman, A. (2006), "Poor Measurement: New Census Report on Measuring Poverty Raises Concerns", Economic Policy Institute, Washington, DC 20005. Online [available] at *www.epinet.org*

Brewer, M., Goodman, A., Shaw, J. and Shephard, A. (2005), "Poverty and Inequality in Britain: 2005", *Commentary No.99*, Institute for Fiscal Studies, London.

Buvinic, M. and Lycette, M. A. (1989), "Women, Poverty and Development in the Third World", In John P. Lewis (ed), *Strengthening the Poor: What Have We Learned,* (Overseas Development Council, 1989), pp.150-61.

Dandekar, V. M. and Rath, N. (1971), "Poverty in India, Indian School of Political Economy," pp.8-18 (Reprinted from *Economic and Political Weekly*, Bombay, Volume VI, Nos 1 and 2, January 2 and 9, 1971).

Dasgupta, P., (993), *An Inquiry into Well-being and Destitution,* Oxford University Press, Oxford.

Datt, G. (1998), "Poverty in India and Indian States; An Update", *FCND Discussion Paper No. 47,* Food Consumption and Nutrition Division, International Food Policy Research Institute,2033, K Street, NY, Washington, D.C. 20006.

Datt, G. and Ravallion, M. (1989), "Regional Disparities, Targeting and Poverty in India", *Working Paper No. 375,* World Bank.

Datt, G. and Ravallion, M. (1994), "Transfer Benefits from the Public Works Employment: Evidence for Rural India", *The Economic Journal*, Vol. 104, No. 427, pp.346 – 69.

Datt, G. and Ravallion, M. (1998), "Why Should Some Indian States Done Better than Others at Reducing Rural Poverty?", *Economitrica*, New series, Vol. 65, No. 257, pp.17-38.

Datt, G. and Ravallion, M. (2003), "Is India's Economic Growth Leaving the Poor Behind?", online [available] *www.ideas.repec.org.*

Datt, G, Kozel V and Ravallion M (2003), "A Model-Based Assessment of India's Progress in Reducing Poverty in 1990's", *Economic and Political Weekly*, January 25, 2003, Vol. XXXVIII, pp.355-61.

Datt, R. and Sundharam, K.P.M (2002), *Indian Economy*, 6th edition, 2002, S. Chand and Company, New Delhi.

Deolikar, A. B. (1988); "Nutrition and labor productivity in agriculture; Estimates for Rural South India", *The Review of Economics and Statistics*, Vol. 70, Issue 3, pp.406-13.

Deolalikar, A. B. and Dubey, A. (2003), "Levels and Determinants of Hunger Poverty in Urban India", Online [available] at *www.worldbank.org/urban/symposium2*.

Deaton, A (2000), "Counting the World's Poor: Problems and Possible Solution". Research Program in Development Studies, Priceton University, NJ, Online [Available] at *www.linkinghub.elsevier.com*.

Deaton, A. and Dreze, J. (2002), "Poverty and Inequality in India; A Re-examination", *Economic and Political Weekly*, September 2002. pp.3729-48.

Demery, L. and Marchant, T. (2002), "Can We Really Measure Poverty". Online [available] at *www.isi.cbs.nl.*

Deolalikar, A. (1988), "Nutrition and Labor productivity in Agriculture; Estimates for Rural South India", *The Review of Economics and Statistics*, Vol. 70, Issue 3, pp. 406-13.

Deshpande, K. S. (2002), "Impact of Infrastructure Created Under Poverty Alleviation Programme (Maharashtra)", Planning Commission, Special Study Reports, Maitree, Aurangbad. Online [available] at *www. developmentfirst.org.*

Dhingra, I. C. (2005), *The Indian Economy; Environment and policy*, Sultan Chand and Sons Educational publishers, New Delhi.

Dubey, A. and Gangopadhyay, S. (1998), "Counting the Poor: Where are the Poor in India", *Sarvekshana: Analytical Report*, Department of Statistics, Government of India, No. 1, 1998.

Dubey, A., Gangopadhyay, S. and Wadhwa, W. (2001), "Occupational Structure and Incidence of Poverty in Indian Towns of Different Sizes", *Review of Development Economics*, 5(1), pp.49-59.

Dubey, A. and Sarma, A. (2000), "Poverty Measurement and Mobility Issues", *Discussion paper*, Center for Development and Community Consulting. GOI, p.6.

Elhance,D.N., Elhance, V. and Agrawal, B.M. (1999), *Fundamentals of statistics*, Kitabmahal, Allahabad.

Fan, S., Zhang, L. and Zhang, X. (2002), "Growth, Inequality and Poverty in Rural China: The Role of Public Investment", *Research Report 125*, International Food Policy Research Institute, Washington, D. C.

FAO Corporate Document Repository (2005), "Nutrition and Poverty: Small-Holder Families", Regional for Asia and Pacific (2005). On line [available] at www.fao.org.

Friel, S. (2004), "Nutrition, Poverty and Health", *National Conference*, North West Ireland, p 4. Online [available] at www.cpa.ie/downloads/publication/conference.

Galbriath, J. K., Conceicao, P. and Kum, H. (2000), "Inequality and Growth reconsidered once again some new evedience from old data", *UTIP Working Paper No. 17*, Paper Prepared for Association for Comparative Studies (ACES), New Orleans, January 5-7, 2001.

Galbraith, J. K. (1979), *The Nature of Mass Poverty*, Harvard University Press, Cambridge.

Garner, T. I., Short, K., Shipp, S., Nelson, C., and Paulin, G. (1998), "Experimental Poverty Measurement for the 1990s", *Monthly Labor Review*, March 1998 p.39-68.

Gedam, R. (1995), *Poverty in India, Myth and reality, Definition and Identifications, Critical Evaluation*, Deep and Deep Publications, New Delhi.

Gordon, G. (2000), 'Measuring Absolute and Overall Poverty', in D. Gordon and P. Townsend (eds.), *Breadline Europe: The Measurement of Poverty*, pp. 49-50.

Government of India (1972), *Towards an Approach to the Fifth Plan*, Planning Commission, New Delhi.

Government of India (1979), *Report on the Task Force on the Projection of Minimum Needs and Effective Demand*, Perspective Planning, Planning Commission, New Delhi.

Government of India (1993), *Report of the Expert Group on the Estimation of Proportion and Number of Poor*, Perspective Planning Division, Planning Commission, New Delhi.

Government of India (1995), *Basic Statistics of North Eastern Region (1995)*, North Eastern Council, Ministry of Home Affairs, Government of India, Shillong.

Government of India (2001), "Nurtitional Intake in India", *NSS Report 471*, 1999-00, p 1, NSS 55th round (July 1999 – June 2000), Ministry of Statistics and Programme Implementation, Government of India.

Government of India (2001), *Provisional population Total; Rural-Urban Distribution*, Census of India, Directorate of Census Operation, Nagaland, p.5.

Government of India (2002), *Central Rural Sanitation Programme*, Ministry of Rural Development, Government of India (Feb.2002).

Government of India (2004-05), "Nutritional intake in India", *NSSO Report 508 and 513.*

Government of Nagaland (1999), *Data Base on Village Level Development Indicators as on 31-03-97,* Directorate of Economics and Statistics, Nagaland, Kohima.

Government of Nagaland (1997-98), *An Economic survey of Nagaland 1997-98,* Directorate of Economics and Statistics Nagaland, Kohima.

Government of Nagaland (2000), *Statistical Handbook of Nagaland 2000,* Directorate of Economics and Statistics Nagaland, Kohima.

Government of Nagaland (2001), *Statistical Handbook of Nagaland 2001,* Directorate of Economics and Statistics Nagaland, Kohima.

Government of Nagaland (2002), *Nagaland Basic facts 2002,* Directorate of Information and Public Relations, Nagaland, Kohima.

Government of Nagaland (2002), *Nagaland, Annual 2002,* Directorate of Information and Public Relation, Nagaland, Kohima.

Government of Nagaland (2002), *Material on Rural Development Programmes in Nagaland,* Rural Development Department, Government of Nagaland.

Government of Nagaland (2004), *Statistical Handbook of Nagaland 2004,* Directorate of Economics and Statistics Nagaland, Kohima.

Government of Nagaland (2004), *State Human Development Report 2004,* Department of Planning and Coordination, Nagaland, p.15.

Government of Nagaland (2007), "Breif history of the District", p.1. Online [Available] at www.wokha.nic.in.

Government of Sri Lanka (2004), *Official Poverty Line for Sri Lanka*, Department of Census and Statistics, Colombo.

Government of Thailand (2002), *Thailand Official PovertyLine*, National Economic and Social Development Board, Bangkok.

Gross, R. (1997), "Nutrition and the Alleviation of Absolute Poverty in Communities: Concepts and Measurement", *Symposium on "Nutrition and Poverty" with a special emphasis on South Asia*, 24th Session of the ACC/, Nepal on 17-21 March 1997, p.2.

Guruswamy, M. and Abraham, R. J. (2006), "Redefining Poverty: A New Poverty Line for a New India", *Economic and Political Weekly*, Vol. XLI No 25, June 2006. pp.2534-41

Haddad, L. (2002), "Nutrition and Poverty", *In Nutrition: A Foundation for Development*, Geneva: ACC/SCN. p.1.

Haq, M. U. (1978), *The Poverty Curtain: Choices for the Third World*, Oxford University press, New York.

Horwitz A (1997), "Poverty and Nutrition in South Asia", The 24th Session of ACC/SCN, Kathmandu, Nepal on 17-21 March 1997, Symposium on *Nutrition and Poverty with a special emphasis on South Asia.*

Hunger Task Force, (2003), *Halving Hunger by 2015: A Framework for Action,* Interim Report, Millennium Project, UNDP, New York.

Islam, R. (1997); "Poverty and Its Effect on Nutrition: Some Question Based on the Asian Experience", p.2. Online [available] at *www.unsystem.org*.

Jamir, K. (2006), "Status of Infrastructure in Nagaland: Strategies to Strengthen Infrastructures for Economic Development", In NUTA (ed.) 2006, *Economic Development in Nagaland, Constraints and Prospects*, p.234.

Jha, R. (2000), "Reducing Poverty and Inequality in India: Has Liberalization Helped?", *Working Paper No. 204,* UNU World

Institute for Development Economics Research. Online [available] at *www.wider.unu.edu*

Jitsuchon, S. (2003), "Poverty Maps Construction in Thailand", Online [available] at *www.unescap.org/pdd/projects/pov_map/7b-Thailand 2003*.

Joshi, A. and Moore, M. (2000), "Enabling Environments: Do anti-poverty programmes mobilize the poor?", *The Journals of Development Studies*, Vol. 37, No. 1, pp.25-26.

Joshi, P. C. (1985), "Poverty Amelioration Perspective", *IASSI Quarterly News Letter*, June 1985, p.14.

Johnson, G. D. (1997), "Agriculture and the Wealth of Nations", Vol. 87, Issue 2, *Paper and Proceedings of the Hundred and Fourth Annual Meeting of the American Economic Association (May, 1997)*, p 1-12. Online [available] at www.jstor.org.

Kannabiran, V. (2005), "Marketing Self-help, Managing Poverty", *Economic and Political Weekly*, August 20, 2005. Online [available] at www.epw.org.

Kapila, U. (2007), *Indian Economy; Issues in Development and Planning and Sectoral Aspects*, 5th edition, Academic Foundation, New Delhi.

Kijima, Y. and Lanjouw, P. (2003), "Poverty in India during the 1990's; A regional perspectives", World Bank Policy Research, *Working Papers 3141*, DECRG, World Bank.

Krishna, A. (2003), "Falling into Poverty; Other Side of Poverty Reduction", *Economic and Political Weekly*, Feb. 8 2003, Vol. XXXVIII, pp.533-42.

Lanjouw, P., Pradhan, M., Saadah, F., Sayed, H. and Sparrow, R. (2001), "Poverty, Education and Health in Indonesia: Who Benefits from Public Spending?" Online [available] at *www.papers.ssrn.com*.

Lipton, M. and Ravillion, M. (1995), "Poverty and Policy", in J. Berhman and T. N. Srinivasan (ed.), *Handbook of*

Development Economics, Vol. III, Elsevier Science, pp.2551 – 52.

Lorant, V., Thomas, I., Deliege, D. and Tonglet, R. (2001), "Deprivation and Morality: The Implications of Spatial Autocorrelation for Health Resources Allocation", *Social Science and Medicine*, Vol. 53, pp.1711-19.

Meenakshi, V.J., Ray, R. and Gupta, S. (2000), "Estimates of poverty for SC, ST and Female - Headed Households", *Economic and Political Weekly*, July 2000, Vol. XXXV No. 30, pp. 2748 - 54.

Meenakshi, V. J. and Vishwanathan, B. (2003), "Calorie deprivation in Rural India, 1983 – 1999/2000", *Economic and Political Weekly*, January 2003, Vol. XXXVIII No. 4, pp. 369 - 75.
Meir, G. and Roucha, E. J. (2002); *Leading Issues in Economic Development*, Oxford University Press, New York.

Milanovic, B. (1998), "Do More Unequal Countries Redistribute More? Does the Median Voter Hypothesis Hold?" *Research Paper*, World Bank, Development Research Group. Online [available] at ww.worldbank.org.

Minhas, B. S. (1970), "Rural Poverty, Land Redistribution and Development Strategy: Facts and Policy", *Indian Economic Review*, April 1970, Reproduced in Minhas, Planning and the Poor, S. Chand and Co., 1978, Chapter II.

Mishra, S. K. and Lyngskor, J. W. (2005), "Poverty, Dietary Imbalance and Sickness among Casual Labourer Households in Shillong (India)", *Working Paper* – May 2005. Online [available] at www.freewebs.com.

Monga, G. S. (1996), *Mathematics and Statistics for Economics*, Vikas Publishing House Pvt Ltd, New Delhi.

Moon, B. E. and Dixion, W. J. (1985), "Politics, the States, and Basic Human Needs; a Cross-National study", *American Journal of Political Science*, Vol. 29, Issue 4 (Nov. 1985), p.661-94.

Morduch, J. (1994), "Poverty and Vulnerability", *The American Economic Review*, Vol. 84, Issue 2, p 221-25. Online [available] at www.jstor.org.

Nair, M. K. S. & Mathew, P. M. (2000), "Poverty Alleviation Programmes and Structural Changes in the Rural Economy", *Special Study Report*, Sponsored by the Planning Commission, ISED, Cochin. Online [available] at www.planningcommission.nic.in.

Nandy, S., Irving, M., Subramanian, S. V. and Smith, G. D. (2005), "Poverty, Child Undernutrition and Morbidity: New Evidence from India", *Bulletin of the World Health Organisation 2005*, 83, pp.210-16.

Navaneetham, K. and Jose, S. (2005), "Poverty, Malnutrition and Mortality in South Asia: A Review of Issues and Options", *CICRED Seminar on Mortality as Both a Determinant and a Consequence of Poverty and Hunger*, Thiruvananthapuram, India, February 23-25, pp.1-21

Oberg, C. (2003), "Impact of Childhood Poverty on Health and Development", *Healthy Generation*, Vol 4, Issue 1, p 1.

Ojha, P. D. (1970), "A Configuration of Indian Poverty: Inequality and Level of Lining", *RBI Bulletin*, January 1970.

Popli, G., Parikh, A., Palmer, R. and Jones (2005), "Are the 2000 Poverty Estimates for India a Myth, Artifact or Real?", *Economic and Political Weekly*, Vol. XL. No. 43. pp.4619-24.

Pradhan, B.K. and Saluja, M.R., (1998), 'An Assessment of Poverty Studies in India with Special Reference to Economic Reforms', *Pakistan Development Review*, pp.10 81-1102.

Pradhan, B. K. and Subramanian, A. (1999); "Structural Adjustment, Education and Poor Households in India: Analysis of a Sample Survey", Paper presented at the World Bank *Workshop on "Poverty Reduction and Social Progress: New Trends and Emerging Lessons; Regional Dialogue and Consultation on WDR2001 for South Asia"*, April 4-6, 1999, Rajendrapur, Bangladesh.

Pradhan, M. and Ravallion, M. (1998), "Measuring Poverty Using Qualitative Perceptions of Welfare", *1998 Conference of the Association of Income and Wealth*, Cambridge, England.

Prabhu, S. (2001), "World Development; Destitution and the Poverty of its Politics", p.7, Online [available] at *www.linkinghub.elsevier.com*.

Prasad, K. N. (1980), *Problem of Economic Development in the Third World: With special references to India*, New Delhi, Sterling Publishers.

Pritchett, L., Suryahad, A. and Sumarto, S.(1999), "Quantifying Vulnerability to Poverty: A Proposed Measure, Applied to Indonesia", *Discussion Paper No. 0610*, Social Monitoring and Early Response Unit, Jakarta.

Ravallion, M. (1992), "Does Undernutrition Respond to Incomes and Prices: Dominance Tests for Indonesia", *World Bank Economic Review*, Vol. C, 1992.

Ravallion, M. (2002), "On the Coverage of Public Employment Schemes for Poverty Alleviation", in Subramanian S. (ed), *Measurement of Inequality and Poverty*, Oxford University Press, p.281.

Ray, D. (1998), *Development Economics*, Oxford University Press, New Delhi.

Safiliou-Rothschild (2001), "Food Security and Poverty: Definition and Measurement", *Working Paper 4*, Online [Available] at www.iwmi.org/dail.

Saith, A (2005), "Poverty Lines versus the Poor: Method versus Meaning", *Economic and Political Weekly*, Vol. XL. No. 43 Oct, 2005. pp.4601-10.

Sen, A. (1981), *Poverty and Famines*, Oxford University Press, Jai Singh Road, New Delhi.

Sen, A and Himanshu (2004), "Poverty and Inequality in India–II: Widening Disparities during the 1990s", *Economic and Political Weekly*, September 25, 2004. pp.4361-75.

Sen, P. (2005), "Of Calories and Things: Reflection on Nutritional Norms, Poverty Lines and Consumption Behaviour in India", *Economic and Political Weekly*, Vol XL. No.43, 2005, p.4611.

Sharma K.C. (1994), *Poverty, Unemployment and Inequalities in Tribal India: With Special Reference to Himachal Pradesh*, Reliance Publishing House, New Delhi.

Singh, C.P. (1989), *Poverty Alleviation Programme under the Plan*, Indus Publishing Company. New Delhi.

Singh, T. B. (2007), "Poverty in Manipur", *Economic and Political Weekly*, Vol. No. 3, Jan 2007. pp.251-254.

Somanathan, R. (2006), "Poverty and Exclusion", *Working Paper*, August 2006. Online [available] at www.econdse.org.

Son, H. H. (2007), "Interrelationship between Growth, Inequality, and Poverty: The Asian Experience", *ERD Working Paper Series No 9. 6*, Economics and Research Department, Asain Development Bank.

Srivastava, S. K., Dutt C. B. S., Nagaraja, R., Bandyopadhayay, S. , Meena, H. R. C., Hegde, V. S. and Jayaraman, V. (2004), "Strategies for Rural Poverty Alleviation in India: A Perspective based on Remote Sensing and GIS-based Nationwide Wasteland Mapping", *Current Science*, Vol. 87, No. 7, 10 October 2004. Online [available] at www.ias.ac.in.

Subramanian, S. and Deaton, A. (1996), "The Demand for Food and Calories", *The Journals of Political Economy*, Vol. 104, Issue 1, pp.133-62.

Subramanian, S. V. et al (2005), "Poverty, Child under Nutrition and Morbidity: New Evidence from India", *Bulletin of WHO*, 2005, p.210.

Tarozzi, A. (2002), *Estimating Comparable Poverty Counts from Incomparable Surveys: Measuring Poverty in India*, Princeton University. Online [available] at www.economia.uniroma2.it

Tarozzi, A. (2002), *The Indian Public Distribution System as Provider of Food Security: Evidence from Child*

Anthropometry in Andhra Pradesh, Princeton University. Online [available] at www.economia.uniroma2.it.

Thirlwall, A. P (2003), *Growth and Development with Special Reference to Developing Economies"*, for Palgrave Macmillan, By Replica Press Pvt. Ltd. Kundli. India.

Todaro, M. P. (1998), *Economic Development*, 6th edition, Addison-Wesley Reading, Massachusetts.

Townsend, P. (1979), "Poverty in the United Kingdom", p.31, Online [available] at *www.archiveshub.ac.uk*.

Vaidyanathan, K. E. (2002), "Measurement of Income Inequalities in Urban and Rural Areas in India", Consultant 3028, Chennai 600040, India. On line [available] www.isi.cbs.ni.

World Bank (2000), "Millineium Goal for World Development" On line [available] at *www.ddp-ext.worldbank.org/ext/MGD/home.do*.

World Bank (2001), *India improving household food and nutrition security; Achievements and Challenges Ahead*, (in two volumes) Vol. II, Annexes Rural Development Unit South Asia Region, *Report No. 20300.*

WHO (2004); "Poverty, disability and community based Rehabilitation (CBR) Programme". UN ESCAP/CDPF *Field Study cum Regional Workshop on Poverty Alleviation Among Persons with Disabilities*, Lanzhou, China, Oct. 2004. Online [available] at www.DAR@who.int.

Webster's New Collegiate Dictionary, (1956), G. & C. Merriam Co., Publishers, Springfield, MA.

Webb, P. (2002), "The Dynamics of Food, Nutrition and Poverty in SE Asia", *Discussion Paper No 9.* Online [available] at www.nutrition.tufts.edu.

Index